Empowering Educators

A Comprehensive Guide to Teaching Grades 6, 7, 8

Linda Berger • Emily Parrelli • Brian Smith • Heather Young

Center for Responsive Schools, Inc.

All net proceeds from the sale of this book support the work of Center for Responsive Schools, Inc., a not-for-profit educational organization and the developer of the *Responsive Classroom*® approach to teaching.

The stories in this book are all based on real events. However, to respect students' privacy, names and many identifying characteristics of students and situations have been changed.

© 2021 by Center for Responsive Schools, Inc.

All rights reserved. No part of this book may be reproduced in any form or by any electronic or mechanical means, including information storage and retrieval systems, without permission in writing from the publisher, except by a reviewer, who may quote brief passages in a review.

ISBN: 978-1-950317-20-2
Library of Congress Control Number: 2021944519

Photographs by Jeff Woodward
Additional photographs by Cory Ryan and Emily Parrelli

Center for Responsive Schools, Inc.
85 Avenue A, P.O. Box 718
Turners Falls, MA 01376-0718

800-360-6332
www.crslearn.org

2nd printing 2021

Contents

Publisher's Acknowledgments v

Introduction 1

1 Developmentally Responsive Teaching 7
- Overview 7
- Grade 6 13
- Grade 7 20
- Grade 8 27

2 Effective Management 37
- Overview 37
- Grade 6 43
- Grade 7 52
- Grade 8 60

3 Positive Community 69
- Overview 69
- Grade 6 74
- Grade 7 81
- Grade 8 90

4 Engaging Academics 97
- Overview 97
- Grade 6 103
- Grade 7 113
- Grade 8 120

5 Connecting With Parents 129
- Overview 129
- Grade 6 136
- Grade 7 143
- Grade 8 152

6 Healthy Teachers, Healthy Classrooms 163

Appendix 198
- Interactive Learning Structures 198
- Interactive Modeling 201
- Logical Consequences vs. Punishment 202
- Responsive Advisory Meeting 203
- Booklists for Diverse and Inclusive Classroom Libraries 204
- Sample Parent Communications 205

References 208

Further Resources 210

Index 212

Publisher's Acknowledgments

Center for Responsive Schools is deeply grateful for the combined talents and expertise of Linda Berger, Kirsten Lee Howard, Julie Kelly, Andy Moral, Emily Parrelli, Jenni Lee Groegler Pierson, Brian Smith, Amanda Stessen-Blevins, Amy Wade, Becky Wanless, Lisa Dewey Wells, and Heather Young. Their hard work, collective wisdom, and collaboration made this series of books valuable resources for other educators.

Center for Responsive Schools would also like to express appreciation to the following people for their involvement in the creation of this book: Michelle Benson, Kevin Bradley, Barbara Findlen, Michelle Gill, Elizabeth Greene, Emily Hemingway, Allison Henry, Cathy Hess, Dr. Lora Hodges, Lindsey Lynch, Jeff Miller, Noelle Serafino, and Anne Sussman.

Introduction

At Center for Responsive Schools, we believe that educating all children is the most important work in the world. But it's no easy task, especially if you're a middle school teacher.

Chances are, you have strong feelings about your own middle school experience. Many people cringe when they look back on those years. The middle school years are marked by significant changes and transitions, including starting a new school, entering puberty, and taking on more responsibility in and out of school. In these preteenage and early teenage years, adolescents explore who they want to be in the future. They experiment with different interests, attitudes, and friendships; they take risks, make mistakes, and closely observe those around them. Middle schoolers are often some of the most honest, humorous, and hopeful learners, which makes them both delightful and challenging to have in a classroom.

As a middle school teacher, you have the honor and responsibility of guiding your students on this journey. It takes a special kind of adult consideration to know when to support middle schoolers, even when they say they don't need you, and when to encourage their independence, even when they don't think they're ready. Maintaining this balance requires constant acrobatics from middle school teachers—an ability that is just one of their many talents.

Who Should Read This Book?

The goal of this book is to help middle school educators do their essential work. Each chapter offers tools, tips, and strategies for building classrooms where all students feel safe, seen, and significant and where educators are empowered to respond to all students' academic, social, emotional, and developmental needs.

To create positive and healthy school and classroom communities, diversity, inclusion, and equity must be at the center of one's pedagogy. Woven throughout these chapters, you will find relevant, impactful practices that can reach every child in every school, every day. All of these practices are based on the *Responsive Classroom* approach, whose six guiding principles form the core of this book. Those principles are:

1. Teaching social and emotional skills is as important as teaching academic content.
2. How we teach is as important as what we teach.
3. Great cognitive growth occurs through social interaction.
4. How we work together as adults to create a safe, joyful, and inclusive school environment is as important as our individual contribution or competence.
5. What we know and believe about our students—individually, culturally, developmentally—informs our expectations, reactions, and attitudes about those students.
6. Partnering with families—knowing them and valuing their contributions—is as important as knowing the children we teach.

Especially in difficult times, these guiding principles remind us of what is most important and motivate us to create classrooms that are inspiring, student centered, and rigorous. All educators, new and veteran ones alike, will find ideas, insights, and innovative approaches in the pages that follow.

How to Use This Book

This book encompasses three different grade levels. We encourage you to read each grade-level section. Equipped with this range of information, educators who teach a single grade level will understand more deeply where their students have come from developmentally, where they are, and where they're going. Educators who teach multiple grade levels, as many middle school educators do, will find valuable information on sixth, seventh, and eighth grades in this book. For ease of use, the book is color coded so you can quickly find the grade you are looking for: yellow for all grades, teal for sixth grade, green for seventh grade, and chartreuse for eighth grade.

You can use this book in many ways. You might want to read the book in order, from cover to cover. You might choose to focus on certain chapters or sections based on your needs and interests, or you might refer to different sections throughout the school year. The chapters are organized in the approximate order in which you might approach your school year planning and are filled with information and ideas that are appropriate at any time.

What You'll Find Inside

Most chapters begin with an overview offering background information and general guidance. Following that, you will typically find sections specific to each grade level. Each section contains useful information that is easily applicable to other grade levels with some minor adaptation.

In **Chapter 1**, "Developmentally Responsive Teaching," you will explore your students' developmental ages and stages to understand more about their developmental journey in your year together.

Chapter 2, "Effective Management," leads you through setting up your physical classroom space and considering the consistent schedule, routines, and procedures you will use throughout the year, while **Chapter 3**, "Positive Community," offers tips, strategies, and approaches for building and maintaining positive community in your classroom.

By **Chapter 4**, "Engaging Academics," it's time to delve into academics, with a focus on engaging all learners, setting high expectations, and guiding instruction based on insights from your knowledge and observations of your students.

The final two chapters focus on the adults in your classroom community. **Chapter 5**, "Connecting With Parents," is a guide to partnering with parents to better support your students and their families. **Chapter 6**, "Social and Emotional Learning for Teachers," focuses on you and what you need to be effective, fulfilled, and flourishing as an educator—all year long, not just after a restful school break!

At the end of this book, you will also find a robust appendix with ready-to-use resources you can incorporate into your instruction right away. You can also scan this QR code for access to numerous additional downloadable resources.

Voices in This Book

This book was written collaboratively by four experienced educators. They blended their decades of teaching experience to offer advice, strategies, and tips that all educators can learn from. The advice and approaches they describe are backed by evidence and research, but just as important, they are also tried and tested by the authors themselves in real classrooms with real students.

Linda Berger

Linda Berger has taught a variety of elementary grades for the past twenty years and has also worked with students in grades six through twelve in interest-based classes. She currently teaches fourth grade at Central Park Elementary in Santa Clara, California. The multicultural community where she teaches provides the gift of diversity. The students understand how the world changes them—and how they can change the world. Linda has written the eighth grade sections of this book, which focus on establishing the practices that will give students greater agency and make their learning matter to them.

Emily Parrelli

Emily Parrelli is a middle school English teacher and *Responsive Classroom* instructional coach in Nashville-area independent schools. She loves being a part of her students' journey as they cross the bridge that is middle school. She has drawn on her own experience and the wisdom and expertise of her wonderful colleagues to write the seventh grade sections.

Brian is the head of middle school at Holy Spirit Episcopal School in Houston, Texas, where he works with fifth through eighth grade students and staff. His favorite thing about working with students this age is the responsibility and opportunity to positively impact a student's life at this time of so much change. Brian wrote the introductions for each chapter.

Brian Smith

Heather Young started teaching in 2011 and is currently a middle school social studies teacher in the Minneapolis metro area. Before her current role, she taught sixth grade reading and reading intervention for six years. One of her favorite things about teaching middle school is being a witness and guide to a powerful period of discovery, mistake making, and growth for students. Heather Young is the voice in the sixth grade portions of this book.

Heather Young

We hope this book will be a helpful resource for you, one that reminds you of the deep value of your work, imparts practical tips and perennial wisdom, and empowers you to teach with hope and joy.

Chapter 1
Developmentally Responsive Teaching

Overview

Imagine you are visiting a classroom where everything appears to be in sync. It seems, at first, that the students are doing all the talking. They are sprinkled all over the room and are working at their own pace on completely different projects. The teacher often takes a step back, observing and coaching as needed, while students guide their own collaborative learning and discussion. As you linger for a while in this classroom, you notice that both students and teacher appear comfortable and at ease, with a high level of interaction among students and between teacher and students. Although it's rare for the room to be quiet or for the teacher to lecture or present to the students, everyone seems to know exactly what to do and how to do it. The room feels busy without being chaotic, familiar while still being respectful.

Perhaps this classroom sounds like many you have seen before, but in my experience, it is the exception rather than the norm in middle schools. Often, middle schools are guided by a set of student expectations, including blanket rules that run throughout the school regardless of grade level. Some of these rules may be appropriate for a specific age group, but students who are at different stages of their developmental path typically do not respond the same way to different classroom environments. All too often we may see a middle school utilizing classroom management techniques that are applied equally to all classes throughout the campus, regardless of the students' developmental needs, classroom community, the teacher's style, and other considerations. When student expectations don't align with student needs, the essential work of a teacher—managing an effective classroom, building positive community, engaging students in challenging academic work, and more—is made much more difficult.

You may be surprised to learn that the chatty classroom described at the beginning of this chapter is an example of a teacher utilizing developmentally responsive teaching techniques with a specific group of students. When we understand who our students are, what our students need, and how to meet those needs, we can create classrooms where all students feel a sense of fun, significance, and belonging. Creating these conditions for student success begins when we understand and utilize developmentally responsive teaching appropriate for middle school students.

What Is Developmentally Responsive Teaching?

Developmentally responsive teaching includes a number of practices and strategies tailored to each student's individual, cultural, and developmental needs and strengths. Gaining a better understanding of the characteristics of each age and grade level helps to ensure our students are valued as individuals while we work toward instilling feelings of fun, significance, and belonging in all.

Sixth, seventh, and eighth grade students are not simply larger versions of their younger selves. Each grade level in middle school is remarkably different from the one before, and students respond differently to the varied classroom and teaching strategies used. Developmentally responsive teaching practices must be underscored by a knowledge of common developmental milestones and tendencies of different ages, as well as an understanding of how to leverage these traits in the classroom. Throughout this chapter, we will describe a range of developmentally responsive practices, with examples and strategies specific to each grade level. We have also included lists of common developmental traits and their implications in the classroom for each grade level, which will be helpful guides to understanding your students' particular developmental stages. This

understanding is based on more than a student's grade and age at a particular time in the school year. It is based on careful attention, cultivated over many hours of observation and interaction, to each student's social-emotional, physical, cognitive, and linguistic development.

What Do Developmentally Responsive Teachers Do?

Developmentally responsive teachers spend time learning about their students, where they come from, what they value, and more. Once teachers understand their students' varied personalities and aptitudes, they continuously assess their students' readiness for different practices and classroom activities, ensuring that all students are appropriately challenged and supported as they grow throughout the school year.

A developmentally responsive classroom produces an environment that supports *all* students. This classroom also takes into consideration the individual needs of students in terms of space and general classroom organization. (See Chapter 2 for more on these topics.) Each class is unique and should be recognized as such with regard to the physical environment where learning is to take place. Beyond establishing the physical characteristics of the classroom, the developmentally responsive teacher utilizes words and nonlinguistic models to meet the individual and collective needs of students socially, emotionally, and academically.

Only through knowing students personally, culturally, and developmentally is a teacher able to create such an environment.

What Do We Know About Adolescent Development?

Adolescence is a time of great change. Over the years, researchers have come to better understand each level of adolescent development, which means that educators have access to evidence-based insights on supporting students in each stage of their growth. To best understand child and adolescent development, there are four key principles (Wood 2017) to keep in mind:

1. **Stages of growth and development follow a reasonably predictable pattern.** In general, the stages of human development extend from infancy to old age. Children progress through the stages of preschool, childhood, young adolescence, and adolescence, achieving developmental milestones in the same general order. Young adolescence is where we find most, if not all, of our middle school students. It is important to note that many of our younger students may exhibit characteristics of the childhood phase while attending a sixth grade classroom. Similarly, some of our older students may begin exhibiting characteristics of older adolescence rather than young adolescence while in their eighth grade year. Understanding where individual students are in the continuum of human development is a valuable tool for academic, social, and emotional instruction.

2. **Children and adolescents do not proceed through each stage at the same pace.** Although children and adolescents progress through each developmental stage in the same order, they do so at their own individual pace. Individual development is influenced by multiple factors. While development happens according to a predictable pattern from infancy through maturity, there are individual differences in the pace of development that can be influenced by individual personality and external conditions such as culture, experience, and socioeconomics. Learning about individual students in order to ascertain their location on this scale of development,

and using that knowledge to inform instructional decisions, allows teachers to become developmentally responsive. Understanding the broad scope of developmental differences helps guide teachers in addressing student concerns, ranging from academics to social-emotional issues.

3. **Children and adolescents progress through the various aspects of development at their own rate.** It is not uncommon for students to progress rapidly through one aspect of development and more slowly through another. For example, some students may present as cognitively mature but socially immature for their age and stage. Other students may be above average in their physical development but have underdeveloped social skills. Middle school is a time of great cognitive and social growth for all young adolescents, and remembering that children pass through various aspects of development at their own rate will help the developmentally responsive teacher to better understand the students in their classroom. In any given class, you will often encounter a wider range of developmental traits than you do chronological ages. Balancing the different developmental stages among all the students in your classroom and, at the same time, meeting each student where they are in terms of their individual progress is the goal of developmentally responsive teaching.

4. **Growth is uneven and can vary within a single student from day to day.** A student may enter your classroom one day appearing socially and emotionally mature and capable, and the next day will exhibit an immature nature that doesn't match their previous behavior and attitude. While this principle holds true at any age, young adolescence is a time when this unevenness is particularly apparent, both to outside observers and sometimes even to the adolescents themselves. Recognizing that it's developmentally appropriate for the same middle school students to enter a classroom on different days with radical changes in their attitudes and behavior can help developmentally responsive teachers adjust their approach and help students maintain their feeling of belonging during the confusing time of adolescence.

A Developmentally Responsive Classroom

As you begin your journey through understanding and adapting to the middle school student, keep in mind that all students will present with different needs, strengths, and characteristics as they journey through their own personal development. That's why developmentally responsive teaching is such a powerful tool. These insights into each individual student, and your entire group, allow you to manage your classroom effectively, build a positive community, and engage in meaningful academics that meet your students' needs and challenge them appropriately. Teachers who use their understanding of childhood development can create a developmentally responsive environment and provide the sense of fun, significance, and belonging that all students seek.

Grade 6

I distinctly remember standing in the hallway one morning during the first week of school as sixth graders filled the space. During these first days of a new school year, students always need help finding classrooms, and more importantly, opening lockers. Moving through the hallway that morning, I looked out at the sea of faces and smiled at the sight of a student who was taller than me, walking next to someone who was quite a bit shorter. Those two students could not have looked more different, but as they walked down the hallway, you could see them, and others, radiating a mix of excitement and nervousness about being in middle school. It was if they were saying, "Look at me, but don't look at me. Talk to me, but don't talk to me. I can do this; no, I can't do this."

This oscillation between seeming opposites is a common pattern among sixth grade students, and it's a developmentally appropriate one. Sixth graders move across spectrums of social and emotional development, from boldness to trepidation, from playfulness to seriousness, and from focusing on peers to enjoying conversations with adults outside their homes. Our students are starting to become self-conscious about their changing bodies, filled with the aches and pains that go with it. Eleven- and twelve-year-olds are beginning to share their ideas and opinions more, sometimes so passionately it may seem rude. It is common for them to start to focus on peer relationships and to need time to talk with their friends. Some challenge the rules and test the limits around them. While these are common characteristics of this age group, these traits will emerge for each student at a different time during your school year. You may look at two students in your class and see two completely different sets of needs. The relationships we build with students, and the time we take getting to know them as individuals, give us the ability to look closer at where they are developmentally and provide the support they need.

Chapter 1 • Developmentally Responsive Teaching

What Sixth Graders Need

As you become more familiar with child and adolescent development and the way these patterns appear in your students, you may begin to notice that there is no "average" student. As teachers, we work to find a balance between these developmentally older and younger students, juggling a variety of individual needs. How do you manage this range when there is only one of you and so many different student needs? Rather than planning for that mythical average student, think about the edges. Consider the students at both ends of the academic, social, and developmental spectrums, and ensure that you provide choices and supports that meet those needs.

Here's how this might look in action:

- **Offer variety in how students get directions.** For instance, a digital assignment might have written directions and an audio recording of you reading those directions out loud.

- **Provide opportunities for students to practice a new skill or content with teacher feedback before asking them to do work on their own.** This connection allows students to take risks in a safe way, building confidence before moving on.

- **Build in student collaboration and debate.** One of my favorite ways to encourage this type of interaction is for students to work as a class to come to a common decision, like determining which three amendments in the Bill of Rights are the most important or narrowing down which community service organizations their class fundraiser should support.

- **Use assessments that address a variety of modalities and learning styles throughout a unit of study.** A student might have the option to write or video record a response in one assessment, while another activity might ask them to respond creatively to a prompt using evidence from what they've learned.

- **Find moments to take a brain break (a quick break to reenergize, reengage, refocus, or find calm) within your class period.** Brain breaks promote young adolescents' academic and social growth by responding to their developmental needs to pause, move, and interact with peers.

Knowing these predictable developmental patterns of sixth grade students allows you to take time to work on creating lesson plans that are developmentally responsive. For example, knowing that students this age enjoy talking to adults outside their home and seeking advice from a trusted adult may lead you to plan more time to build relationships with your students. Ask your students questions and make connections with them. Be open to sharing a little about yourself so they can get to know you. Many educators work to strike just the right balance here. For me, it means I am open to conversations about my love of *Hamilton* and *The West Wing*, growing up on Harry Potter books, the newest treat I've baked, and my pets. It's about sharing enough information for students to get a sense of who you are, without sharing every detail of your personal life. These conversations also help model the skills of setting and respecting boundaries.

Making Mistakes

One area that's important to address every year is mistake making. Eleven- and twelve-year-olds typically begin to become defensive of their mistakes. Normalizing making mistakes, referring to mistakes as a part of the everyday school experience, is a way to ensure that sixth graders accept the risks and pitfalls that come with learning and growing. The first few weeks of school offer a perfect opportunity to build this mindset into your class culture. You can discuss mistakes during academic tasks, and you can also make dealing with mistakes a game.

Show students that mistakes are expected and can be corrected. On particularly challenging assignments, one of my colleagues encourages her students to "make good mistakes and be brave in your attempt." She uses the power of her words to shift the common conception around mistakes from blunder to bravery, helping allay students' worry about how they are perceived by their peers.

> **The Maze Game**
>
> Years ago, a colleague introduced me to the Maze Game. Here's how it works. On a giant tarp, tape out a grid with squares large enough for a student to stand on comfortably. The number of squares can vary based on the needs of your group, but a 5 × 5 grid is a good place to start. On a piece of paper only you can see, draw a map of a secret path the group needs to discover. Then, ask students to take turns trying to find the correct path through the maze. Moving one square at a time, students guess whether they should move forward, diagonally, or to the side. If they get it right, they keep going; if they get it wrong, they go to the back of the line. For the first round, students cannot talk or help each other in any way. In the second round, using a new path, they can use nonverbal cues. The third time around, they can use words. During the debrief, we talk about which round was most successful, and why. Often, students recognize that making a mistake—learning which step wasn't the right one—actually helped their classmates find the right path, and that working together and supporting each other made the process easier and more fun.

As sixth graders connect with their peers and their teachers and become more comfortable with making mistakes, they will inevitably make behavior missteps. It is crucial to apply the same developmentally responsive framework when handling any discipline concerns that arise. Early in my teaching career, I had a particularly talkative class. It felt as if I was constantly telling students to stop talking and return to work, which took away from my instructional time. For certain students who continued talking after my reminders, I had to follow up with a consequence. The frequency of these frustrating moments ultimately corroded my relationship with some of my students. Looking back now, I realize I was missing the signal they were sending me: these eleven- and twelve-year-olds desperately needed time to talk with one another that our schedule wasn't providing. I now take time in my lesson planning to consider where I can build in structured student-to-student interaction to meet the students' need for connection and my need for their focus on academic tasks. When classrooms reflect students' developmental needs, students are more active and engaged, and there are fewer behavior concerns.

Social and Emotional Learning

The social and emotional needs of our students should also be part of our planning as we weave social and emotional learning skills into our lessons. Small-group work is one of the strongest tools for supporting students' social and emotional learning skills while remaining developmentally responsive. Sixth grade students enjoy their peers but still need practice in strengthening their cooperation skills. Providing structured opportunities for peer-to-peer interaction meets students' need for connection as well as the goals of our instruction. Small groups also offer a safe space for students to practice assertiveness. Using an interactive learning structure offers your students a clearly defined way to interact within a lesson or class period. One of my favorites is Think-Pair-Share. In my sixth grade classroom, I introduce this interactive learning structure by explaining how to find a partner and what steps to follow. (One student shares their thoughts, the partner asks a follow-up question, and then they switch.) I then pose a question to my class and give them sixty seconds of think time. Finally, I remind students of the pairing method I'm using (perhaps finding their "sole partner," or someone wearing shoes that look like their own) and how much time they have. This interactive learning structure is a quick, fun way to meet students' needs for processing time, movement, and social interaction, all while filling a need in the instruction.

See the appendix, p. 198, for more on this and other interactive learning structures.

Final Word

The transition sixth graders make from elementary to middle school marks an important time in their life. As a sixth grade teacher, you will play an important role in guiding your students to become independent, confident learners. As you look at the sea of faces in front of you, remember to see the individuals and not just the collective group. Being developmentally responsive in your planning and instruction will help each sixth grader succeed.

Sixth Graders

Common Characteristics	School Implications

Social-Emotional

• Are very social and engaged with peers; heavy users of social media.	• Offer structured opportunities to practice social negotiation and cooperation, with adults ready to step in when needed.
• Can seem impulsive; may talk before thinking.	• Provide opportunities to discuss and modify rules and routines as students' interest in fairness grows.
• Enjoy the challenge of competition and team activities.	• As the level of challenge and competitiveness increases, encourage participation by focusing on effort rather than perfection.
• Have a growing interest in and excitement about the wider world, including past and current events.	
• Can be moody and sensitive.	• Create avenues for exploring history, biography, and current events.
• Learn well in collaborative groups.	• Incorporate collaborative groups in lesson plans; change the composition of these groups as needed to adjust the social mix and address inclusion and exclusion concerns.
• Are highly aware of issues of inclusion and exclusion.	
• Are self-focused and interested in imagining themselves in adult roles.	• Provide opportunities for students to be leaders and mentors to children in younger grades.

Physical

• Are restless and very energetic.	• Provide lots of opportunities for exercise and snacks!
• Girls may experience an early adolescent growth spurt and sexual maturation, and some boys begin rapidly growing taller.	• Build in quiet breaks during the day for needed physical rest.
• Need lots of food, sleep, and physical activity.	
• Begin to exhibit improvement in motor skills, although clumsiness may continue.	

Sixth Graders

Common Characteristics	School Implications
Cognitive	
• Would rather learn new skills than review or improve previous work. • Have trouble making decisions and are defensive about mistakes. • Becoming more adept at abstract thinking and deductive reasoning. • Enjoy the challenge of reasonably hard work and increased responsibility. • Are increasingly able to see the world from different points of view and perspectives of other cultures. • Like to challenge rules, argue, and test limits. • Are interested in learning about older and very young people. • Enjoy challenging tasks, but might need help with time management and homework skills.	• Allow students to undertake scientific study, mathematical problem-solving, and invention. • Offer real-world opportunities for learning life skills like writing letters, interviewing community figures, or participating in local organizations. • Provide opportunities for students to engage in "adult" academic tasks such as interviewing, footnoting, internet research, long-term reading assignments, and real-world applications of probability and statistics. • Incorporate adult empathy, light humor, and sensitivity into your interactions with your sixth graders, which can help them cope with their maturing minds and bodies. • Provide opportunities for cross-age tutoring and mentorship to foster interest in other age groups and support students in resolving conflicts. • Establish firm and fair rules and logical consequences for items lost and tasks left undone.
Language	
• Enjoy arguing and debating; appreciate humor. • Imitate adult language. • May show interest in and facility for languages, music, or mechanics.	• Provide opportunities to engage in authentic, safe argument and debate. • Provide more challenging and sophisticated writing tasks, especially ones that pique their personal interest and that allow them to experiment with topics like blood and gore, romance, and fantasy.

The information in this chart is based on *Yardsticks: Child and Adolescent Development Ages 4–14*, 4th ed., by Chip Wood (Center for Responsive Schools 2017) and Child Development Guide by Center for Development of Human Services at SUNY Buffalo State (New York State Office of Children and Family Services 2015).

Grade

Anyone who has worked with middle schoolers might describe these years of development as "two steps forward, one step back, one step forward, three steps back." Nowhere is this more acutely felt than in the seventh grade classroom!

Numerous contradictions characterize seventh graders. Their peers are most important and influential to them, but they can also be incredibly socially awkward. They have a great, emerging interest in global issues but can struggle to have genuine empathy for their classmates. They cling to their independence and yet are easily embarrassed and overly concerned with being part of the group.

These fluctuations happen in the classroom, as well. Imagine this typical seventh grade scene. One student shares a lovely example of a metaphor while another student catapults their pencil across the room. A seventh grader loudly complains, "This is so hard—I don't get it!" You look at the student's paper and see that it is blank, but as the two of you begin to discuss the topic, you realize that the student does understand, and reluctantly, puts pen to paper. A student who frequently participated in class discussions now refuses to say even a single word, all because of a new and dreaded addition: braces.

What Seventh Graders Need

Working with seventh graders can be a complicated dance, and it is all about balancing developmental differences. Remember, you might have eleven-year-olds and thirteen-year-olds in the same classroom; in other words, some students are just exiting childhood while others are very nearly teenagers. Their developmental needs will differ and change throughout the school year. At times, it feels as if they change week by week or even day by day!

As you get to know your students, keep these developmental needs of seventh graders in mind:

- **Seventh graders are emerging as global thinkers and thrive when they are allowed to serve their community and make a difference.** They will enthusiastically dive into a unit on social justice issues or the history of civil rights movements. They enjoy participating in service-learning projects that serve their local community, such as holding a canned food drive or visiting a nursing home. Another idea is to organize clubs around issues that interest them, such as recycling or pet adoption.

- **While they have compassion for global issues, seventh graders can simultaneously lack empathy for their peers.** Set firm expectations for behavior and social interactions and remind students of these expectations often. For example, before class presentations, remind students to be respectful and engaged listeners. If students make a behavior mistake, redirect them clearly, quickly, and kindly so expectations are held up. (See Chapter 3 for more information on redirecting language.)

- **Seventh graders are eager to participate in conversations about serious topics such as drugs, alcohol, sex, violence, and family problems.** However, they may lack the ability to talk about these issues appropriately. Providing safe spaces for them to share their thoughts and opinions, such as in an advisory setting, gives them the opportunity to practice and take risks under the guidance and modeling of a caring adult.

- **An emerging skill for seventh graders is their increasing ability to work on long-term projects and assignments.** They thrive with the added responsibility and complex outcomes, but they need support along the way to be successful. One way to support students is to set a goal or learning outcome from the beginning. Set due dates, benchmarks, or checklists throughout the project or assignment to help students learn time management. Use exemplars, even if you have to make them yourself. Seventh graders are beginning to see something of value in the work they produce, so knowing where the bar is helps them to know where to begin.

- **Similarly, seventh grade is an appropriate time to introduce students to major assessments, such as unit tests, exams, state testing, or standardized tests (such as PSAT/SAT or ACT).** The stakes for assessments can feel high for seventh graders and can be the source of great anxiety for them. It is helpful to talk about positive character traits such as grit, a growth mindset, and the ability to separate personal worth from academic performance.

While the ups and downs of seventh grade can seem daunting, there are two essential tools to successfully working with seventh graders: establishing routines and requiring accountability. Seventh graders can be unpredictable and hard to read. By setting predictable routines, we can create safe spaces for them to explore boundaries and different social relationships. Additionally, seventh graders want to be given greater responsibility, which they perceive as a sign they're entering adolescence. Setting clear expectations and holding students accountable to those expectations is one way to foster the development of responsibility in and out of the classroom.

Establishing Routines

Routines are the regular procedures students take part in as they go about their school day. Routines include turning in homework, walking to lunch, cleaning their band instruments, or putting on their PE clothes. The key to making routines a normal, effective part of the day is to model them with clear, straightforward steps.

In my second year as a middle school teacher, I had an "aha" moment about modeling routines. The desks in the classroom were arranged in groups of four to align with seventh graders' eagerness for social interaction and to foster collaboration. While I loved the way the table groups worked, the untucked chairs after the bell rang were a nuisance and made it difficult for the next class to navigate the room. No matter how many times I reminded my students to be responsible for their desk, many chairs would still be untucked when students exuberantly departed for their next class. One day, it occurred to me that perhaps they didn't know what was expected of them as they left the room. I'd reminded them to be responsible many, many times, but I'd never actually *shown* them what

I meant. The next day, I did just that, following the four steps of Interactive Modeling. It felt ridiculous at first, but as I was moving through the steps, I noticed that the students were fully attentive. We followed up with a discussion of the steps, and it was clear that the message had been received. Best of all, there was not a single chair untucked when they left the room at the end of class! After that day, there were usually one or two students who needed reminders, but now I had a point of reference for holding them accountable.

See the appendix, p. 201, for more on Interactive Modeling.

Holding Seventh Graders Accountable

Accountability, or holding students to the expectations you set for them, is another important tool in our seventh grade teacher toolbox. With our seventh graders, accountability is the primary way to teach responsibility. The first key to accountability is in setting the expectation. For example, after I modeled the routine of tucking in chairs for my students, the expectation was clear to them: *this* is how we prepare to exit the classroom. Next, students need reminders and reinforcement of their behaviors. Because they are increasingly taking responsibility for their learning, seventh graders benefit from knowing when they are (and are not) on the right track with their behavior and academic performance. Another key is to remember that having empathy for students does not mean releasing them from accountability. As educators, we need to be empathetic, and we are often tasked with exercising our empathy with seventh graders! However, we should also remember that we best serve our students when we can be honest about their behavior, academic performance, and social interactions. Holding them accountable for their actions is vital in developing their social and emotional competencies.

Social and Emotional Learning

While routines and accountability help target key social-emotional skills in our seventh graders, it is also essential to consider how we can accommodate their developmental needs. For example, knowing that social interaction is a primary driving force, we can leverage it in the classroom. Great cognitive growth occurs through social interaction. By facilitating guided social interaction, we can reduce social anxiety while helping students to develop positive social skills. In the seventh grade classroom, we might use interactive learning structures to support students in these connections. For instance, a small group of students could use Jigsaws, where each member of the group is responsible for sharing a piece of the learning with the others. Another option could be Think-Pair-Share, where each student is required to carefully listen to their partner's ideas so they can share them with the class.

See the appendix, p. 198, for more on these and other interactive learning structures.

Final Word

The seventh grade classroom has the distinction of having the most variance in terms of development. While this range can pose unique challenges for the adults in seventh graders' lives, leveraging these developmental characteristics can help bridge the gap between childhood and adolescence. Remembering to implement routines and hold students accountable will help foster their positive growth and development.

Seventh Graders

Common Characteristics	School Implications
Social-Emotional	
• May try on different personalities as adult personality beginning to emerge. • May begin to push boundaries and test limits. • Are capable of self-awareness, insight, and empathy; are more reasonable and tolerant. • Have a keen, emerging awareness of and interest in global and social issues. • May make new friendships with classmates they have not been friends with before. • Are enthusiastic and spontaneous, and appear to feel secure; can be both playful and serious. • Can get caught up in the moment and be influenced (positively and negatively) by their peer group. • Care greatly about peers' opinions; may hesitate to open up in a larger group due to worry about how peers will perceive them. • Abound in leadership qualities.	• Offer opportunities to discuss and modify rules and routines as appropriate, while maintaining consistent, clear, and calm adult authority. • Design projects that allow students to explore solutions to local and global concerns. • Allot time for peer conferencing and partner projects; honor choices of subject matter and work partners when possible. • Start with small-group work and build up to larger group interactions. • Inform students about opportunities for cross-age tutoring, jobs at school, hosting visitors, community service, etc.
Physical	
• Are very energetic; need lots of exercise, sleep, and food. • Have growth spurts; may be fidgety or uncomfortable, and may need to move around more than sixth or eighth graders do. • Understand the idea of training and regular exercise as a means to improve physical ability.	• Schedule regular breaks and structured transitions throughout the school day and within class periods. • Provide regular opportunities for students to move around and stretch. • Help students create routines and practice for follow-through. • Draw parallels between students' extracurricular activities and their schoolwork (for example, making the connection between going to basketball practice and winning a basketball game to show how homework and class participation contribute to academic success).

Seventh Graders

Common Characteristics	School Implications

Cognitive

• Are increasingly able to plan and organize thoughts, work, and goals; can handle lengthy homework assignments spread over several days, though these can be problematic if they extend over weekends. • Begin to demonstrate ability to think abstractly about complex moral issues. • May begin to excel at a subject (such as science) or a skill (such as drawing). • Able to see both sides of an argument, but still like to argue one point of view. • Will initiate their own activities without adult prompting; like to invent games.	• Teach students how to use weekly or monthly planners. • Provide students with opportunities to participate in service-learning projects or clubs around issues that interest them (with adult guidance and support). • Integrate students' interests into lesson plans by using cross-disciplinary teaching models. • Use formal debate structures to provide meaningful opportunities for students to listen to different perspectives and explore current events, civics, and history. • Listen and respond to student suggestions for changes in routines, when realistic.

Language

• Understand and enjoy wordplay and more sophisticated jokes; like to try out new vocabulary. • Enjoy conversation with adults and peers; gaining confidence in their ideas and opinions. • Enjoy trying out the latest slang from music and pop culture.	• Introduce activities that allow students to learn vocabulary roots and explore new languages. • Provide opportunities for students to engage in active debate and discussion; support these activities with lessons teaching students how to agree and disagree respectfully. • Guide students on appropriate use of slang, including when and where it is considered acceptable (for example, appropriate to use in a text message, but inappropriate in an essay).

The information in this chart is based on *Yardsticks: Child and Adolescent Development Ages 4–14*, 4th ed., by Chip Wood (Center for Responsive Schools 2017) and *Child Development Guide* by Center for Development of Human Services at SUNY Buffalo State (New York State Office of Children and Family Services 2015).

Grade

Picture eighth graders on the first day of the new school year. They need to figure out how to navigate their new role—they're in the top grade, they know they're the big cheese, and they're practically in high school. At the same time, they're still kids and often find themselves lost ("Am I in the right room?"); uncoordinated ("Ouch!" "Oh, sorry!"); immature ("Stop. Making. Fart. Noises."); dramatic ("Help! It's a SPIDER!"); smelly ("Who forgot deodorant?"); and very, very sweet. Welcome to the adventure! As a teacher of eighth graders in a developmentally responsive classroom, you facilitate an equitable learning experience that allows breadth and fosters flexibility, one that enables students to feel recognized as individuals rather than as names on an attendance sheet. You work to reframe developmental qualities into strengths (except maybe not the smelly one!) and create a deep and lively learning environment in which everyone is accepted.

What Eighth Graders Need

The need for peer approval is a benchmark of this age. Although eighth graders crave attention from adults ("Cute shoes!" "What's your favorite team?" "Do you have any cats?"), their peers often take precedence over all else. It's possible to use both of these characteristics to create a strong, positive foundation for the year. Starting on the first day of school, you can immediately establish trust in the most basic way by welcoming each student on their own terms (perhaps with a handshake, high five, or wave). An important piece of establishing trust with eighth graders is assuming the best about these students, a clean slate that leaves previous behaviors in the past where they belong. To build this trust throughout the year, it's essential that every student interaction we have is authentic. Because eighth grade students are exquisitely sensitive to emotions, they often sense inauthentic responses, like fake interest. A second of our attention and focus ("How did yesterday's concert go?"), extended early in the day, pays back dividends in establishing real relationships. What students say and do will sometimes be at odds with how they feel, but they will know you care. With those few seconds of connection, we meet their need for recognition and security, and an equitable and productive school day is off to a great start.

Since appearance to peers or saving face is everything in eighth grade, students often hesitate to reveal they don't know something lest they be seen as uncool or weak. Phrases you may hear, such as "This is boring," may actually mean "I don't get it." To add an important layer to our foundation of trust and connection, it helps if we prepare the environment for students so they know what to expect. Provide classroom elements as simple as an accessible visual schedule, a class norms poster, and project timelines to answer important questions students may not feel comfortable asking yet and to help them gain equilibrium in a new class. Carefully arranging the physical environment will facilitate the developmental need eighth graders have to move; leave space between seating and, when possible, set desks up in pods or groups. Those small touches create an unspoken message that you have given thought to your students' needs. (See Chapter 2 for more on setting up your classroom space.)

Building Trust

See the appendix, p. 203, for more on Responsive Advisory Meetings.

Even when we are prepared, there will still be times when we forget our students' developmental needs. The first time I walked into a class of eighth graders, I left an important piece of my developmental learning at the door. Rather than being nervous, I was instead eager and excited to start our time together building community. Naturally, I assumed, a silly skit during the first Responsive Advisory Meeting would make perfect sense, right? Wrong. (So very, very wrong!) It was simply too soon for these students to take that social risk and be vulnerable with their peers. While I remembered to set up an appropriate physical space, I forgot my students' emotional and social needs. While they were (grudgingly) willing to participate, it was not the connecting activity I envisioned because any initial trust they might have credited to me was lost. My error made the activity a disconnecting experience for students, instead of building community.

I learned my lesson. For the next few weeks, I worked to regain trust and credibility with the students, one step at a time. In my particular case, I directly addressed the misstep with the class, admitted my mistake, and got their feedback on better ways to move forward. One strategy that helped was to quickly identify the student I call the "herd turner," a class leader who can influence others to follow them, a role you often find in eighth grade groups. I got valuable input both from that student and from the class. More important, I acted on that input, which created some trust.

At this age, students' growing desire for independence needs to be encouraged, modeled, and practiced in developmentally appropriate ways. As the teacher, it was my job to talk less and listen more, to invite students *into* the conversation rather than talking *at* them. In this case, I engaged my students by implementing the important practice of voice and choice. Engaging eighth graders makes them feel seen and heard and provides opportunities to offer opinions (voice) and exercise independence (choice).

The class regrouped with practices like student-designed projects and class closings that integrated questions designed to grow their self-awareness, such as "What is one thing that moved your learning forward today?" and "What is one bright spot your group discovered?" Eventually, we even incorporated increasingly riskier activities into Responsive Advisory Meetings—but only after we allowed ourselves time to develop a safe social environment.

Embracing Independence

Middle school teachers understand that their students' burgeoning independence impacts the school experience. They thus need to design multiple opportunities to integrate collaboration into classroom activities that will allow students to develop important speaking and listening skills. The more traditional model of a teacher-driven classroom often misses opportunities for students to practice the flexible thinking and peer compromise that are well within reach for eighth graders. That is why spending time early in the year to prioritize community and connection is so valuable. I call it "Go slow so you can go fast." With support and modeling, our students can use collaborative groups to productively communicate and compromise with peers. This foundation of social awareness makes the transition to heavier academic content remain student centered and supports valuable life skills.

I once saw an amazing lesson on literary identity called "Who Am I?" The lesson, which engaged students in an in-depth exploration of Mary Shelley's *Frankenstein*, utilized a breakout puzzle experience. To make this breakout activity successful and encourage the types of open-ended questions critical to the development of flexible thinking in eighth graders, trust was established within the academic community through months of incorporating practices like positive teacher language and interactive learning structures. The teacher assigned students to small groups to solve word puzzles, analyze passages in the book, explore geographical directions, investigate historical figures, and more, all in the context of the academic lesson taking place around the room. It was all purely content driven, with no busywork at all. Each group was assigned to collect clues from their task and to coordinate with the other groups to combine the data and discover the solution to the breakout puzzle. This lesson became a celebration, a rich culminating activity that brought together weeks of layered earlier lessons connecting social and emotional competencies like cooperation and assertiveness with academic content that explored multi-dimensional characters and social commentary. It provided valuable opportunities for students to move, discuss, collaborate, discuss, resolve conflicts, and record learning independently.

Social and Emotional Learning

It can take a while to find the sweet spot as we work to develop ways to both connect with students and model important social behaviors. Students don't need us to be their friend. They need us to be a trusted, consistent adult role model. That includes modeling ways to own mistakes. These small yet powerful strategies provide both security and agency to students who learn to understand that they really do have influence on their own direction—and that you're there to support them.

Once a social-emotional foundation is firmly established, it's possible to introduce more academic lessons. We can initially do this with a whole group, direct instruction model before releasing students into smaller collaborative groups. The model of I Do, We Do, You Do (first you model a skill, then students model it, and finally everyone does it together) looks slightly different with this age. As we've covered in this chapter, you will likely have a variety of developmental levels—social, maturity, academic, language, independence, and more—within your class. When moving your class into small groups, it's important to balance these developmental levels in order to address students' sense of fairness, establish an equitable model, and maintain a sense of self and respect for the community. It instills an expectation that everyone's contributions will count, that important element of voice and choice.

Although students may recognize a need for this collaborative equity work, they are still learning the social skills needed to implement it. Using

See the appendix, p. 201, for more on Interactive Modeling.

the practice of Interactive Modeling, teachers can initially demonstrate academic behaviors highlighted in eighth grade, such as asking for clarification, engaging in deeper content analysis, and addressing social commentary, and then gradually allow students to practice and apply these behaviors within the class's balanced collaborative groups. The good news is that peer connections provide the exact framework that can help students learn from each other. We just need to remember that students this age can be loud. Very loud. Still, they also have a need for quiet and reflective time. This active time–reflective time instructional strategy can be enhanced by establishing efficient learning areas throughout the classroom environment that provide space for small groups to settle and that allow students to meet their physical and social-emotional needs. With a little prework to help everyone in the class develop these social-emotional and academic competencies, the teacher demonstrates trust in the students, allows them to learn in their own way, and remains available to coach them through areas of need—all important ways for students to develop agency in this stage of emerging maturity.

Final Word

Rich learning experiences like the one described above are well within reach in eighth grade. They allow a teacher to create groups that meet the developmental needs of the class, address a variety of academic targets, and meet eighth graders' need for challenge. The investment of time to get to know students and build community at the beginning of the year is paid back in valuable learning dividends throughout the school year. Students will remember these meaningful academic lessons and the valuable integrated curriculum they tackled with their peers. The life skills they experience are important bonuses, frosting on an already rich cake.

Eighth Graders

Common Characteristics	School Implications
Social-Emotional	
• Pay close attention to peers, who mirror what's in and what's out.	• Balance independent and group times to honor eighth graders' dueling desires for unstructured (but still monitored) socializing and introspective time.
• Are concerned with personal appearance, but are generally unconcerned with the neatness of their personal spaces.	• Observe closely, listen carefully, and encourage safe risk tasking to help combat increased self-consciousness and the tendency to withdraw.
• Are moody and sensitive; may shut down and withdraw or suddenly flare up in anger.	
• Can easily have their feelings hurt, and can easily hurt others' feelings (frequent meanness may stem from being insecure or scared and from not wanting to be left out).	• Allow students to choose partners or group members, but monitor the tone and process of collaborative work carefully. Assign partners if needed.
• May need more support when working in groups.	• Structure opportunities for students to engage in constructive criticism of each other's work, as well as self-evaluation.
• May begin to form close friendships at this age; often form cliques or small groups.	• Plan service projects like food drives or community cleanups.
• Spend hours using social media or playing video games.	
• Worry and complain about schoolwork and homework.	
• Increasingly punctuate their humor with sarcasm.	
• Are often quiet and secretive.	
• Are interested in issues of fairness and justice; want to serve others.	

Eighth Graders

Common Characteristics	School Implications

Physical

- Have lots of physical energy; need as much physical activity as possible.
- Often have skin problems; hygiene is becoming more important.
- Most girls are menstruating and have reached almost full physical development; most boys are showing first signs of puberty (they will reach full development at fourteen or fifteen).
- Are often embarrassed by health and sex education classes, as well as PE (including dressing and showering), leading to silly or rude behavior.
- Many students show a strong interest in sports.

- Provide brief periods of activity outdoors or frequent brain breaks in the classroom.
- Encourage participation in team sports and activities as a safe way to explore new interests.

Cognitive

- Show continued growth in abstract reasoning—making assumptions, developing hypotheses.
- Are often tentative, worried, and unwilling to take risks on tough intellectual tasks; will challenge teachers by asking, "Why do we have to learn this?"
- Express likes and dislikes more emphatically (for example, may love math and hate English).
- Think about many sides of an issue or solutions to a problem.
- Like to challenge intellectual as well as social authority, often for the sake of argument.
- Can think globally, but often can't put ideals into practice in day-to-day life (for example, are concerned about social justice issues, but may often be mean to each other).

- Offer chances to take safe intellectual risks, like thinking of a range of solutions to a problem or identifying multiple possibilities about what caused it.
- Have short, regular, predictable homework assignments directly related to the next day's assignments; allow students to check homework in small groups at the beginning of the school day, which builds academic collaboration.
- Provide opportunities to balance teacher evaluation and grading with self-evaluation of schoolwork through rubrics they help create.
- Provide opportunities to consider and debate many sides of an issue.
- Connect with students by offering calm and thoughtful responses.
- Invite students to participate in classroom governance, plan activities and events, or tutor younger children as a way to make real-world connections to their global thinking.

Eighth Graders

Common Characteristics	School Implications
Language	
• Sometimes shut down and answer adults' questions with a single word, but might just as likely respond with loud, extreme language.	• Offer calm, thoughtful responses to outbursts. • Take student opinions seriously. • Engage students in finding solutions to their concerns.

The information in this chart is based on *Yardsticks: Child and Adolescent Development Ages 4–14*, 4th ed., by Chip Wood (Center for Responsive Schools 2017) and Child Development Guide by Center for Development of Human Services at SUNY Buffalo State (New York State Office of Children and Family Services 2015).

Chapter 2
Effective Management

Overview

Let's revisit the developmentally responsive classroom we observed in Chapter 1, the classroom where students felt safe and comfortable, experienced a social connection through learning, and knew what to do in their shared space. How did the students come to feel so comfortable and know exactly what to do in this particular classroom? From the first day of school, their teacher incorporated developmentally responsive teaching techniques. And now if you were to observe the students closely, you'd see them entering and exiting the room in an orderly fashion. Each morning the teacher greets the students and makes connections as they enter. Students drop off their homework in specific places and settle into their seats for their classroom activities. If students arrive late or miss a day, they know exactly what to do when they return. No instructions seem to be given, and yet the class starts smoothly. Even with a high level of movement, social interaction, and cooperative learning, students remain mostly focused and on task, sharing the space thoughtfully with only a few quick reminders from the teacher.

The techniques discussed in this chapter, combined with proactive and reactive discipline strategies, help teachers lay the groundwork for this level of effective management in real life. This chapter offers support for the effective management of middle school classrooms, including balancing different personalities, arranging the physical environment of the classroom so that it supports the curriculum and students' academic progress, and even managing time appropriately. Many effective management techniques and strategies rely upon the way we speak to students and present ourselves; positive teacher language will be introduced in this chapter and further explored in Chapter 3.

Discipline strategies, both reactive and proactive, also play a major role in establishing a well-managed classroom. To manage classrooms effectively, we must teach behavior as well as academics. In fact, the word "discipline" is derived from the Latin word *disciplina*, one of whose meanings is "instruction." As educators, we help guide our students to learn and practice self-discipline so they begin to develop internal motivation, grit, and self-control rather than behaving as a result of a teacher's external intervention. We teach these skills for self-discipline, always with an understanding of where our students are developmentally, so our students can learn and practice what they need for success. In this chapter, we'll focus on reactive strategies, or ways to respond to behavior mistakes in the moment so that students return to a successful trajectory. We will also discuss discipline in more depth in Chapter 3.

What Does Effective Classroom Management Look Like?

Certain key practices help to create a calm, orderly environment that promotes student self-sufficiency and allows students to focus on learning. Teachers effectively manage classrooms when they:

- **Organize the classroom for safety and autonomy.** A classroom with clear expectations for student safety lends itself well to the promotion of autonomy. When teachers manage the physical classroom environment carefully, students feel a sense of familiarity, dignity, and comfort within their own learning environment. This sense of dignity, or feeling of worth, honor, and respect, helps students develop the confidence to do what is needed when they need to act.

- **Arrange the classroom environment for maximum learning.** Learning objectives also need to be taken into consideration. A classroom with clear procedures for academic purposes helps to increase the sense of belonging we wish to instill in our students. When students feel like they belong in the class community, positive behaviors are likely to increase.

- **Establish and reinforce clear routines and procedures.** Early establishment of routines and procedures is essential to creating a classroom environment that is managed effectively. Many middle school students will be unfamiliar with the routines and procedures of middle school: How do you enter the classroom? How do you turn in homework? What do you do if you have been absent? All of these routines, and more, can be established early in the year, so that students will always know what to do. And when we use proactive strategies to decrease indecision we see a reduction in misbehavior, and even difficult moments begin to feel manageable. When we build relationships with students and increase their sense of belonging and significance, misbehaviors decrease.

- **Communicate clear behavioral expectations and respond to misbehavior respectfully.** Our proactive routines and procedures will provide the structure that most students will need to find success in a classroom. With clear structure and opportunities to practice, students will quickly learn to follow certain procedures, which can help eliminate confusion, build confidence, and head off many behavioral problems early on. Despite this structure, we will need to respond to misbehavior at times, and we have quite a few tools to help us accomplish this. We will next look at three logical consequences that are essential to maintaining order in our well-managed classroom.

> **Classroom Routines for Middle Schoolers**
> - Entering and exiting classrooms
> - Turning in homework
> - Catching up on work missed while absent
> - Moving furniture (stacking chairs, making desk clusters, and so on)
> - Using materials and equipment appropriately
> - Knowing what to do during transition times
> - Using lockers
> - Asking to use the bathroom
> - Working with a partner
> - Knowing how to offer feedback to a classmate
> - Submitting late work
> - Volunteering to answer a question

Logical Consequences in Middle School

As we work toward establishing an effectively managed classroom, we may utilize logical consequences for our students in order to redirect behavior toward positive and productive directions. Logical consequences are a set of strategies we can use to respond to misbehavior that teach students to take responsibility for their actions while allowing us, as teachers, to meet three goals. First, they allow us to set clear limits. Second, they hold our students to a high standard of behavior. Third, they provide respectful, related, and realistic responses to misbehavior.

See the appendix, p. 202, for more on logical consequences vs. punishment.

Importantly, punishment is *not* a logical consequence. Whereas logical consequences help students see how their actions impact others, thus teaching them how to respond differently the next time, punishment sends the message to students that they, not the mistake they made, are the problem. This negative message can be internalized over time, leading not only to decreased academic performance but also to student reliance on evading consequences or being dishonest to avoid punishment.

Punishment can be one of the greatest promoters of inequity in schools. Research by scholars like Michael J. Dumas and Joseph Derrick Nelson (2016) and Rebecca Epstein, Jamilia J. Blake, and Thalia González (2017) demonstrates how students of color are significantly more likely than their peers to experience punitive disciplinary practices, both in school and outside of it. Using logical consequences that are respectful, related to the misbehavior, and realistic not only helps our classrooms to be safer, calmer places, it also goes a long way to building a positive sense of self, internal motivation, and the ability to recognize and regulate one's thoughts, emotions, and behaviors.

The three logical consequences are:

- **Loss of privilege.** We use this logical consequence when a student's behavior does not meet preestablished expectations during a time when they have the privilege of acting autonomously. The student loses that privilege for a brief time, usually a class period or a day, before they have another opportunity to manage the privilege responsibly.

- **Break it, fix it.** This logical consequence is used when a student's mistake, carelessness, impulsivity, or forgetfulness results in damage. Break it, fix it simply repairs a problem that occurred when the student made a mistake, with an emphasis on the opportunity the student has to make right what went wrong.

- **Space and Time:** Used to help students who need to regain self-control by moving to a different location (space) to have a few minutes (time) to reflect and reset, all while preserving the smooth flow of the classroom.

These key practices are further discussed in the grade-level sections following this introduction. Each logical consequence is appropriate for all middle school students. You can turn to the sixth grade section to learn more about Space and Time, the seventh grade section for break it, fix it, and the eighth grade section for loss of privilege.

Through intentional teaching and modeling of routines and procedures, teachers can create a classroom environment that proactively reduces off-task behavior and supports student learning. The classroom community benefits as students recognize that they can moderate their own behavior and take ownership of their learning and academic success.

Meeting All Students' Needs

Understanding your students' diverse cultural and developmental needs, as discussed in Chapter 1, provides the foundation for a classroom environment where students are guided by routines and procedures and corrected in respectful ways. Giving students an opportunity to take part in the establishment of the classroom community, expectations, and procedures further enhances the inclusive nature of the classroom. Students bring their own perspectives to the community, and sharing these perspectives helps make their own sense of belonging more profound. This give-and-take also reinforces their sense of ownership within their own classroom.

As we take this inclusive approach, each classroom will look somewhat different, but the core concept will remain the same. Students, as unique individuals, can work together to develop and grow with their teacher's guidance and within the environment that is needed to support all in the classroom community.

Teacher Language and Leadership

Beyond understanding our students' cultural and developmental needs, we must also consider how our leadership style and our use of teacher language impact the classroom.

How do we lead our students so we model the behaviors and practices we encourage them to try? How does our language set the stage for behavioral and academic success? A teacher's leadership style is the manner and approach a teacher takes in supervising students and the classroom space, motivating students, and executing administrative tasks, duties, and procedures. Teacher language is the professional use of words, phrases, tone, and pace. The combination of these elements creates a classroom environment that empowers all students to confidently engage with the curriculum content, learning activities, new ideas, and each other.

We encourage a community of positive interactions, responsibility, accountability, and trust in our classroom, and effective management is the foundation of a classroom culture in which students behave respectfully toward themselves, others, and property. Ultimately, our language and leadership style send messages of consistency, safety, and expectations for respectful communication and interactions among all students and their teachers. We will discuss teacher leadership and teacher language more fully in later chapters, but it is important to keep them in mind as we work to design and implement our effectively managed classroom.

• • • • • • • • •

In the sections that follow, you will dive more deeply into what effective management looks like in grades six, seven, and eight and how you can set up both your classroom and your students for success. You will find practical tips and ideas specific to the grade level you teach by turning directly to that specific section. However, all of the sections contain helpful, relevant information for middle school teachers, so it is worth reading all three sections. In particular, you will find more details about investing students in the rules in the sixth grade section, employing envisioning language in the seventh grade section, and working with colleagues to establish appropriate routines in the eighth grade section.

Grade

Effective management is an important factor in the success of your sixth grade students. In most middle schools, sixth grade is the transition year from elementary school. Students are going from only a couple of teachers a day in elementary school to perhaps up to eight teachers in middle school. That's eight different ways to enter or exit a classroom, turn in a paper, sharpen a pencil, get a tissue, or find a partner. As your students learn to navigate a larger school and take on more responsibility, you can set your classroom and your students up for success through effective management strategies. Taking the time to organize your space in a way that encourages autonomy and student focus, teaching behavior expectations, and responding to mistakes in a way that quickly and respectfully helps students return to learning will result in a positive and productive classroom environment.

Organizing Your Space

When I started my first year of teaching, one of the things I was most excited for was having my own classroom. How would I arrange the student desks? Where would the teacher workspace be? Would there be bulletin boards? How would I decorate the space? As you think about effective classroom management, the first thing that comes to mind may not be the physical arrangement and organization of the room. But the setup of your room can play a large role in the day-to-day function of your class. If the physical space is arranged purposefully, students feel more comfortable in the environment.

Each school year, I set aside a couple of days to get the classroom space ready and organized. It is important to me that the room not only is functional but also feels comfortable for students. This initial setup time allows me to try different placements until I feel confident in the room arrangement, but I also make sure that it is possible to adjust with student input once the year begins. When I first enter the space, I take a few moments and stand in the front of the room, imagining the various scenarios that are bound to unfold: students working on their own or in small groups, grabbing supplies they need; the phone ringing during a lesson; or myself grading papers that students have handed in. With these and many more scenarios in mind, it's time for the setup to begin.

The easiest starting point for me is where my teacher space will be. I prefer a clear line of sight to the classroom door, student desks, and the room as a whole. Once my corner is set, I focus on student movement in several areas I know they need access to: their seats, supplies, and some open space.

- **Student seats.** Sixth grade students benefit from working in small groups so they can practice their assertiveness and meet the need for social interaction. Whichever layout you choose, be mindful of how you can partner and group students for interactive learning throughout the lesson without causing too much disruption.

- **Student supplies.** When possible, I like to keep supplies on an open bookcase, near the trash and recycling bins, by the door. This location means that students are not opening and closing cabinets, as sometimes they aren't aware of how loud their bodies and voices can be. Having supplies and the trash can in the same place means a student can grab a tissue, throw it away, sanitize their hands, and get a pencil, all in one stop. This system minimizes movements that might cause distraction for others.

- **Open space.** In sixth grade, it is important for students to get up and move a bit and to have time to interact with their peers. Leaving some open floor space allows room for brain breaks, interactive learn-

> **Classroom Supplies**
>
> Schools vary in what supplies are provided and which ones a teacher may choose to get. You may consider having markers, colored pencils, scissors, tape, glue sticks, tissues, hand sanitizer, and pencils. (It's remarkable how many pencils middle schoolers go through.) Clipboards are also useful for holding paper and pens so that students can use them as writing tablets when they are sitting on the floor or moving around the room.

ing structures, a place for groups to work, a different study area during independent work time, or an area for a Responsive Advisory Meeting, all without rearranging furniture.

See the appendix, p. 203, for more on Responsive Advisory Meetings.

An additional physical space to set up may be an area for Space and Time, a strategy that provides a nonpunitive way to help students regain self-control but still maintains the overall flow of your classroom. When students feel unfocused, particularly if emotions are distracting them from the task at hand and they need a break, they can get up and head to the Space and Time area. In general, it is better for only one student to use this space at a time, although occasionally, if students are sufficiently mature, two may use it at once. Once there (space), they take a couple of minutes (time) to breathe and refocus, and then they return to their seats. In our classroom, there is a picture of a beach, a two-minute timer, a stress ball, and a Hoberman sphere, although tools are not necessary for Space and Time to be successful.

Classroom Displays

As you finish setting up the physical arrangement of your space, you'll begin to think about the visual elements that aid in effective management. One visual way to support your sixth graders is to have a central location for important information. In our classroom, this "student center" is a bulletin board near the classroom supply station and door. It has a copy of the bell schedule, grading scale, lunch menu (one of the most popular requests), club information, and team announcements. Clearly mark the space, and explicitly tell your students what resources are available there. When there are so many new things to manage in middle school, this single repository of information can be reassuring to any nervous sixth graders. A larger bell schedule and copy of your class expectations in an easy-to-see location is also helpful in effectively managing your class.

There are a couple of other things to keep in mind as you think about the visuals of your room. We want sixth graders to see themselves in every aspect of the classroom, from the books in the library to the posters on the wall. Work to represent the diversity of your students around the space. If you maintain a classroom library, give students a survey to see what type

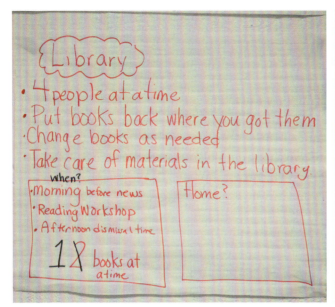 

See the appendix, page 204, for resources for developing a diverse classroom library.

of main characters they'd like to see. Do your best to find those books, and get them in the hands of students. As you put up posters, think about the message you are sending to your students about their place in your room and in that content. A science teacher colleague of mine has posters of female, male, Asian, Black, white, and differently abled innovators in science and math all over their classroom. The message is clear: everyone has a place in science. As you search and create these visuals, ask your colleagues for ideas, or tour some of the other classrooms in your building.

Schedules, Routines, and Procedures

You and your students rely on daily schedules, routines, and procedures, important patterns that create the backbone of our school days. When we explicitly teach routines and procedures and ensure that our schedules maximize students' developmental characteristics, we set our students, and ourselves, up for success.

Schedules

Typically, middle school teachers do not have much control over the school day schedule, but there are still scheduling considerations within your lessons. Thinking back to developmentally responsive teaching, we know that our students need movement. Movement can reenergize and refocus the brain for the eleven- and twelve-year-olds in front of us. Find a space in your lesson for a quick brain break, remembering that these can be as short as one minute. Sixth graders also benefit from scaffolded opportunities for peer interaction during lessons. While eleven- and twelve-year-olds love socializing, they aren't yet able to use time with their peers to interact and learn simultaneously. Interactive learning structures provide quick, easy-to-use frameworks for lively learning that meet students' needs for movement and interaction and teachers' needs for engagement in learning.

Routines and Procedures

When your classroom is arranged and the visuals are in place, it's time to think about the more behavioral aspects of effective management. One place to start is with the routines and procedures students will encounter while in your classroom. When your sixth graders are not clear on routines or procedures in a space, whatever confidence they may feel at the start of the day can quickly turn to nervousness. Sixth grade is a period of big adjustment for them in terms of management and responsibility, so anything we can do to support students ultimately helps our classroom management as well.

See the appendix, p. 201, for more on Interactive Modeling.

To prepare, imagine yourself as a student in the classroom, and make a list of the different routines that may come up throughout a class period as well as your preference for how they are done. For instance, I tell my students, "Turn in all assignments in the turn-in basket labeled for your class. My hands are not the best place for it." This small routine is something I model for them at the start of the year: *Walk to the stack of baskets, find your class bin, front of the paper up, in the basket, return to your seat.* This clear routine, handled the same way every single time, gives students the consistent structure they crave at this age.

Using Space and Time appropriately is a routine I teach and model early on in the school year. Students are directed to turn the timer on and use any of the tools there to help them refocus. When the time is up, they self-check to see if they are ready to return to their seats, and usually they are. The idea is to help students to take a minute when they feel distracted or sense the pressure rising, before it overflows like a shaken can of soda.

Space and Time is also a chance to model self-regulation. I can vividly remember one day when my third-hour class proved to be a particularly challenging one. As my fourth-hour class got started, I could feel that I had not reset and needed a minute. I told my students honestly, "Sixth graders, I am feeling like I'm not quite in the right space to start this lesson. I need a quick moment of Space and Time before we start. Please get out your articles and preview the text." I stepped to my desk, grabbed my coffee, and took a few sips along with some deep breaths. Then I walked back to the front of the room, regained their attention, and started the lesson. My behavior showed students that adults also need to self-regulate and sometimes take a break. Space and Time is a norm, not an exception.

These routines and procedures might seem basic, but you can't assume that sixth graders coming into your class will know how to do all of the things on your list, and on all their other teachers' lists, without being shown how. Take the time to explicitly name, model, and practice these routines. While it may feel like a waste of precious instructional time, it will pay off down the line. Effective management is rooted in building student autonomy and responsibility. When students know the routines and how a room "works," they have one less thing to be concerned about. They can focus on learning and being part of the classroom community.

> **Teaching Routines With Colleagues**
>
> Consider starting a conversation with your sixth grade teaching colleagues, especially if your school has a team teaching model. Where are there opportunities to streamline the routines in your space? Can you all use the same method for bathroom passes? Perhaps each of you can agree to start your first class of the day making sure students have all the supplies ready for the day. Think how much time you could save each other later in the day by taking these few minutes in the morning!

Classroom Management and Responding to Misbehavior

Building an effective learning community takes time and effort, but there are two important tools for this work that you will use every day: classroom rules and teacher language. Managing your classroom, responding to misbehavior, and focusing on learning all happen much more smoothly with clear expectations and positive teacher language.

Investing Students in the Rules

When it comes to creating and displaying classroom expectations, I purposely use the word "expectations" rather than "rules." Expectations have positive connotations, and send the message that you believe in your students' abilities to meet them. Rules are something that can be broken, and often have a negative connotation related to punishment. Set yourself and your students up for success with positively worded, brief, direct, overarching expectations. In an ideal world, you would work with your students to create these rules to set the tone for your class community. However, as a middle school teacher with multiple class sections, you may find the idea of creating expectations with input from each section too much to think about at the beginning of the year, and having multiple lists of expectations on the wall could get confusing.

Consider this alternative: at the start of the year, I ask each of my classes what classroom expectations would help them feel successful. I tell them that I will be doing the same activity with each class section. The next day, I take a few minutes to show the students all of the lists, and the students in each class work to connect and condense the five lists to find commonalities. We discuss the importance of respect and how that can play a role in our expectations. Finally, on the third day, we take ten minutes to look over the final common list and discuss whether we can agree to these expectations. Over the last few years, my classes have come up with expectations that include "respect yourself," "respect others," "respect the environment," and "follow school expectations."

Make sure the classroom expectations are clearly posted and are something you refer back to often. For instance, imagine you are about to have students move around the room to do a project involving a multitude of supplies. You might take a moment to ask the students, "Which of our class expectations will be especially important during this activity?" If you are taking your class to an assembly, you might ask, "What will our class expectation of respecting others look like while we are at this assembly?" These prompts remind students what they should be doing and get them started with the right foot forward.

Teacher Language

A middle school teacher often teaches five daily classes, each averaging 25 students, for a total of 125 students a day. From greeting them as they enter class, answering a question during a lesson, or having a conversation before class starts, the number of teacher-student interactions in a single day is well into the hundreds. Effective management relies on your use of language, and with so many conversations and interactions throughout the day, you can see why it's an important part of classroom management.

Positive teacher language is clear, direct, and brief. It focuses on action and conveys faith in your students' abilities. Think about the difference between saying, "Jamie, why are you walking around right now? That's not what you should be doing," and "Jamie, sit in your seat." The intention of both phrases is to get Jamie back to their seat. In the first, Jamie is singled out in front of their classmates, with attention drawn to their negative behavior. The second statement is meant to get Jamie's attention and briefly redirect them to what they should be doing while maintaining their dignity. Brief moments can convey impactful messages. Compare "Good morning, kids," with "Good morning, scientists!" The first greeting sounds like the teacher is addressing a young class, while the second helps students envision themselves as scientists before they even make it to their chairs.

Another way to use teacher language is to proactively manage possible misbehavior. Imagine it's October, and you are about to transition your sixth grade students to find a partner in the room, share something they learned from a reading, and then return to their seats. Where could this go wrong? Proactively addressing concerns with positive teacher language might sound like this: "You are going to stand up and find a partner you haven't talked to today. You will have three minutes to share. The person with the shortest hair will go first. Remember to share the mic so you both have a chance to share your insights. Listen carefully to what your partner says so you can share out with your table. I will let you know when the time is up."

In this set of directions, you've clearly laid out the expectations for students. There is little room for confusion in how they should partner and what they should do. When students know what is expected of them, they are more likely to meet that expectation than to get off track.

Teacher language is something we can always work on. With hundreds of interactions with students every day, there are going to be times we make a mistake, or think later about how we could have more positively phrased our redirection of a student's behavior, or helped students envision what they are doing so they find success. Being aware of our words and tone and recognizing those moments for growth make a difference; you never know what sticks in the minds of your students.

Final Word

Even with all the preparation of your physical classroom arrangement, use of visual supports, establishment of expectations, and practicing of routines, there will be a need to respond to misbehavior. The students in your room, after all, are still eleven- and twelve-year-olds. Their brains are still developing, and hormones and impulse control can overwhelm them. Focus on using effective management strategies to create a safe and predictable learning environment for your students, and watch your sixth graders begin to define themselves as individuals because of the structure and community you create.

Grade

Effective classroom management requires us to have developmental awareness and plenty of patience. When approaching classroom management in the seventh grade classroom, I remind myself that developmentally, seventh graders need plenty of elbow room *and* lots of social interaction. We have to think about how we can simultaneously give them space and make them feel like they are part of the group—a balancing act, to be sure! The question I ask myself at the beginning of every school year is, "Where should I start?"

Organizing Your Space

Before students arrive for the first day of school, I begin with setting up the physical space of the classroom for success. Ideally, students are arranged in small and intentionally organized groups of three to five. This works well whether they are seated at tables or at desks pushed together in a collaborative configuration, such as a circle or a square. Even if the classroom is arranged in rows or students sit in pairs, students still benefit from having structures in place to make partnering up or forming small groups low risk. Along these same lines, seventh graders also love sticky notes, individual whiteboards, or hand signals for nonverbal communication; they can participate in class by sharing their thoughts and ideas (of which they have many) without having to speak.

> ### Forming Small Groups
> It takes thought to create small groups of seventh graders that can be cooperative and responsible. As you form student groups, consider how their abilities, interests, and background knowledge connect with the goal and nature of the work they will be doing. Whatever strategy you use for forming groups, it's helpful to review expectations clearly and provide guidance for collaboration so everyone can be successful.

We also want to consider providing a space where students can express their creativity, such as a graffiti board, a messaging board, whiteboard space for doodles, or a "burning questions/comments" chart. Seventh graders love to experiment with different styles of handwriting and lettering. They also enjoy sharing their increasing interest in humor with adults and classmates alike. I have a colleague who has dedicated a section of his whiteboard for this purpose; his students bring in printouts of their favorite (and school-appropriate) jokes, memes, and doodles. This collage is a simple way for his students to bring in humor and fun to their own classroom space. Remember, of course, that seventh graders will test boundaries; it's a good idea to have a set of rules and expectations for using a community space and to check in on these spaces often.

When it comes to supplies, seventh graders either feel completely possessive of them or never have them. They can also be careless and reckless with classroom supplies (ruler sword fights, anyone?). I find modeling how to use supplies and setting specific guidelines for accessing them, using them, and putting them away helps to minimize problems. I also set aside five to ten minutes for cleaning up before the end of class when we are using materials, which helps teach students responsibility and has the added bonus of maintaining my personal sanity. You might even give students sets of supplies to work with and then have them return the supplies as a set—this helps keep track of those glue stick caps!

Quick Tip

Providing individual supplies is expensive, especially when the burden of cost often falls on the teacher. Have a "sanitizer bucket" where students can place supplies they are returning. Use a sanitizing solution to rinse the items and leave them to dry on the counter overnight.

Classroom Displays

As you think about organizing your classroom, consider how you will make the most of its walls, including frequent-use space (for example, a whiteboard or projector), semiused space (perhaps a TV or calendar), and rarely used space (think of the poster that has been on the wall since you moved into the classroom). One of my favorite features is the blank space on the walls at the beginning of the year. I always make sure there is room to add student work, photos, and visuals for our current units, and I change these displays periodically. So often, we put up great posters on the walls and they quickly become wallpaper. Think about how this space can function as a practical way to foster community and inclusion in our classrooms. When we display student work grouped together, it shows that our students are part of something special and that their work is worthy of sharing with the wider community.

An example that comes to mind is a project my seventh graders complete toward the end of the school year, after we have read myths and legends about knights. We study the art of heraldry and each student creates their own coat of arms; it's an opportunity for the students to make choices about who they are as individuals (something we know seventh graders love) while also doing something highly structured (something we know seventh graders need). I hang their work on a bulletin board outside our classroom, and it's always a delight to see them bring their friends over to see their personalized work and make connections to or learn something about their peers through the imagery.

Schedules, Routines, and Procedures

One of the great things about seventh graders is that we can capture their attention in increasingly longer spans of time as compared with sixth graders. However, it is still advisable to include scheduled breaks in their day and even during their class periods. Middle schoolers in general tend to lose interest after a set amount of time, so I typically include brain breaks and transitions in my lesson plans. A lesson plan like this might begin with a five-to-ten-minute opening activity reviewing learning from the previous day, continue with a brain break, then transition into small-group learning for the rest of class, and finally conclude with five minutes back in our seats to answer questions, go over the homework, and clean up.

Classroom Management and Responding to Misbehavior

The way you manage the day-to-day ups and downs in your seventh grade classroom is key to building a positive learning community for your students. Having clear, high expectations for all students, using teacher language to bolster group and personal identity, and responding to misbehavior with logical consequences are tools you can use every day to be the consistent, firm, and empathetic teacher your students need.

Having Difficult Conversations

In my experience, one of the most difficult challenges with seventh graders is what can be nicely called "antagonism" and not so nicely called "attitude." This behavior can manifest in many ways, including in our interactions with students. For example, one week you can carry on a pleasant conversation with a student, and the next week they seem shocked and embarrassed that you would want to talk with them! The key is not to take it personally (even though *they* seem to take most things personally); this type of behavior is normal and expected at this age. Remember that developmentally, seventh graders are going through a roller coaster of changes, including physical, hormonal, social, emotional, and cognitive. What we work toward is helping them grow *out* of this phase. Some tips for navigating seventh graders' conduct include keeping a calm, neutral demeanor; giving them space when they need space; allowing them a chance to start over (with guidance on your expectations); and talking honestly about their behavior.

With seventh graders, it's helpful to be honest in our communications so we can build trust and help students grow from their mistakes. For example, a common problem I come across in seventh grade is exclusive behavior. I once had a homeroom class that included a group of girls who would gather separately when it was time for us to do a whole-group activity, specifically leaving out the other two girls in the class. It took a series of difficult conversations with them about why their behavior was inappropriate and hurtful in order to get them to change. I like to tell students, "You don't have to be friends, but you do have to be friendly." This mantra helps them to understand that while they are not expected to be friends with everyone, they are expected to treat others with kindness and consideration.

Break It, Fix It

Seventh graders can often be unpredictable and difficult to read, so it is especially important to consider your tone and delivery when it comes to responding to misbehavior, as they will respond in kind to your emotional energy. It is much more effective for you as the disciplinarian to use a neutral tone and to be firm, consistent, and fair. It's also important that we have faith that students want to do better and can do better. In the sixth grade section of this chapter, we discussed Space and Time as a valuable structure for our middle school students. While students can choose for themselves when they need to use Space and Time, there are two strategies we as educators can pull from our disciplinary toolbox: break it, fix it and loss of privilege. (See the eighth grade section for more on loss of privilege.)

Break it, fix it works exactly the way it sounds: you made a mistake, and now you need to make it right. Here are some examples of what this might look like in the classroom:

- **Break it:** A student colors on their desk.

    Fix it: They wipe their desk with a cleaning solution to erase the markings.

- **Break it:** A student breaks a beaker during a science lab.

  Fix it: They borrow a pan and broom from the custodian to clean up the shards of glass.

- **Break it:** A student insults a classmate.

  Fix it: They acknowledge that they've caused hurt feelings and apologize.

- **Break it:** Students were disruptive and difficult with their substitute teacher.

  Fix it: They apologize for their actions and make a plan for behavior expectations that you will hold them accountable to during your future absences.

A few thoughts and tips about using break it, fix it:

- **The goal is to teach personal responsibility and to do so in response to something that *can* be fixed.** If it can't be fixed, this might be a situation for something like loss of privilege.

- **Students should only be responsible for the problem they create.** If you as the teacher can identify only one student among others who have made a mess, don't make that one student clean up after the others.

- **Give yourself time to respond appropriately.** When something breaks in the classroom or students begin to argue, our response to the situation will determine the outcome. In that moment, we need the situation solved. Save a conversation or discussion about the situation until after the problem has been fixed; this breathing room allows both you and the students time to calm down, properly assess the situation, and prepare for a conversation.

Developing Identity Through Envisioning Language

It may not seem obvious at first glance, but our language plays an important role in classroom management. By using envisioning language, we are providing for our students' safety and well-being; in return, students are more likely to be cooperative and engaged. What we say, how we say it, when we say it, and why we say it are all contributing factors in proactively preventing misbehavior and responding appropriately and effectively when misbehaviors do occur.

> **Envisioning Language**
>
> Envisioning language encourages students to visualize a goal and a path to achieving it. When teachers use envisioning language, their words encourage students to see themselves positively, as proficient learners, capable problem-solvers, and valued members of the classroom community.

Envisioning language is a tool we can use to foster positive group and personal identity and to make students feel a sense of belonging and significance. It also helps students build confidence and positive mental images of themselves, which is something they can struggle to do on their own. Seventh graders are beginning to realize that they are individuals distinct from their peers, and while this can be something they embrace, it can be a source of great anxiety in equal proportion. Here are some examples of the envisioning language I use in my own classroom:

- "I see that everyone has their homework out on their desk. You read the daily announcement for instructions on what to do at the start of class; you're demonstrating our class expectation about being ready."

- "We're starting our next unit today. There might be some things that are new to you and will require hard work, but we showed with our last unit that we're more than capable of taking on new challenges!"

- "Teams that collaborate make the best use of their class time; discuss with your group how you can be great collaborators as we work on this project."

Final Word

A colleague of mine with years of experience working with middle schoolers succinctly summarized effective management in the seventh grade classroom:

> Seventh graders make me a better teacher because I really have to be on top of my game to get through to them, and sometimes I fail. I have a tough cohort this year, and I have been firm, direct, and fair with them. Even so, when they see me, their eyes light up. They are happy to see me, and this lets me know they respect this in their teachers. If I am getting this from this group of seventh graders, I know I am on the right track. To put it in simpler terms, seventh graders are honest—they tell us what they need if we are willing to listen and pay attention.

Though it may be challenging at times and our patience may be tested, we know that our students need guidance and direction. Effective management helps us to reduce problem behaviors so we can enjoy the wonderful excitement for the world, curiosity in learning, and rapid growth in our seventh graders.

Grade

Remember the first time you watched preschoolers play? They are optimistic ("This is fun!"), connected ("Where is my place in this group?"), assertive ("It's *my* space!") people who work every angle to discover their boundaries. Sounds like eighth graders! One enjoyable transition we can see our students making as they enter this new grade is that they are becoming more purposeful in taking care of themselves and each other. How does a developmentally responsive teacher support their students in seeing their place in this learning adventure? We start at the beginning, working *with* them to design a classroom community that takes their needs into account and makes sure they have the agency to contribute, autonomy to make mistakes, and opportunity to always improve.

As we discussed in Chapter 1, eighth grade bodies and minds are growing at warp speed. Eighth graders need room to move. Although they may look like adults, research tells us the frontal lobes of their brains need several more years to become fully enough developed to govern their decision-making. As their teachers, we work with them to design an environment to accommodate this reality and set them up to be successful. Organization and routines are the structures that pull the classroom community together. The more student agency and opportunity eighth graders have, the better their connections with each other and with their learning. Harnessing the desires for ownership and empowerment are natural ways to manage our eighth grade classes.

Organizing Your Space

In an ideal situation, our classroom allows for flexible design. By nature, I'm a minimalist. For the first decade of my teaching career, I routinely cleared out a piece of furniture from my classroom each year. After several years, all that was left were group tables, a few bookshelves, seating, and my pared-down desk. While this philosophy may not work for everyone, it sure did for us. What we invented was open space. So much open space!

In my case, that room design allowed my students to move around, access materials, spread out along the floor, sit in multiple spaces with their friends . . . just be. As a teacher, it can be liberating to clear out the clutter that so quickly envelops a classroom. Keeping your space simple and organized brings focus to what you really need in your teaching area. For the students, open space means that they can be comfortable in the classroom and can easily rearrange desks and materials to make the space into whatever is needed that day. Need space to film a video, stage a scene from a play, or hold a class meeting? You can do all three in one class period without breaking a sweat, as long as your space is flexible enough.

Tips for Classroom Arrangement

- **Open space:** Wide aisles, space between desks or tables, and open areas allow our students to move safely and gather in small groups for project work.
- **Student supplies:** To avoid traffic jams, use basic community supplies (pencils, rulers, tagboard, markers) set in a few spaces around the room.
- **Seating:** When possible, a variety of seating options (cushions, chairs, stools) support crucial student agency and meet a physical need to move.

Classroom Displays and Resources

For students to feel a sense of comfort and ownership in their shared classroom space, it's important for them to see themselves and their peers reflected in the displays and resources around them. Plan for the majority of classroom displays and learning charts to be student created, and leave plenty of room on the walls for student work. Student-created displays foster pride in ownership, reflect the learning that has occurred, and invest students in their environment. An added benefit of this approach is, truthfully, that students look at the displays they and their peers have made more often than they look at teacher-created or store-bought materials.

Intentionally curating a diverse classroom library is another way to work toward the important goal of supporting students in feeling a sense of ownership. What our students read is a way to show they exist. To elevate this idea, it's essential that any library contain materials that reflect both the students and the world around them.

See the appendix, p. 204, for resources for building a diverse classroom library.

The material chosen for our class libraries can also both engage and connect to the timely real-world issues they care about. For example, as middle school teachers, we know this is an age where social issues become important to our students. "What does it have to do with me?" soon pivots to "What impact can I have?" Books can offer compelling connections between your curriculum and real-world issues. In recent years, a wealth of resources have been developed to support our students to become not only skilled learners, but better people. The books we choose empower our students as they see changemakers in whom they can see themselves.

Schedules, Routines, and Procedures

With eighth graders, it is important to design a classroom that reflects the world around them. Once we set the foundation of functional routines—routines that create procedural structures—we can turn our attention toward starting routines that foster connection, comfort, and learning.

Schedules

The period and block schedules in middle school are a switch from the day-long schedules of the elementary world. Fortunately for us, our eighth graders have had two years to become accustomed to this arrangement. And truth be told, our students prefer the faster-moving pace as it keeps things more interesting for them. The challenge for educators is to create time for students to check in with each other on a regular basis: daily, weekly, or whatever consistent time a short meeting can be held.

In our jam-packed days, the minutes we take to interact with our students during scheduled gatherings—what schools may call advisory, tutorial, homeroom, or something else—form crucial relationships. Implementing a Responsive Advisory Meeting during this time creates a predictable, consistent routine to build belonging, significance, and fun. With a meeting like this, students first come together as a class community to start their day. This whole-group time encourages them to think about and participate in their classroom community. It would be so easy for students at this age to fall into an egocentric trap. Our community routines keep them developing empathy as a practice for the rest of their lives.

See the appendix, p. 203, for more on Responsive Advisory Meetings.

Routines and Procedures

Structures and routines create safety, consistency, and normalcy for students because the students themselves understand and contribute to them. For the most part, these necessary routines involve explicit teaching of related skills that support three critical competencies—learning, organization, and responsibility:

- **Learning:** "Do I feel a part of this learning community?"

  Example of related skill: How do I enter the classroom and sit down?

- **Organization:** "Am I prepared?"

  Example of related skill: Do I know where to find the materials I need?

- **Responsibility:** "What do others need from me?"

  Example of related skill: How do I disagree with someone?

While schoolwide consistency is important in some things, there can be variation in certain norms. Talk with grade-level colleagues to create some agreements around routines to create useful structures that will grow consistency and comfort for your shared students.

With students this age, one approach that is particularly useful to integrate into your routines is the use of nonverbal signals. Eighth graders are loud. They have a lot of energy, and they truly can't keep it bottled up all day—so don't expect them to! Instead, institute some nonverbal signals that are easy to see and remember, such as raising a hand for attention, pinkie-thumb shake for agreement, or a chime sound for quiet. Music is also a lovely way to gain attention and to foster a predictable transition signal. Just choose a consistent song and get student input on it. All of these options help to balance classroom expectations so that eighth graders have an opportunity to be their rambunctious selves when appropriate and then quickly return to a decibel level more conducive to schoolwork.

Whatever routines you and your teaching partners decide are important, it's helpful to:

- **Prioritize.** While there are many skills that are nice to have in a student, decide which ones are important to you and are essential for the start of the year.

- **Model, model, model.** Use the practice of Interactive Modeling to ensure your students know exactly what is expected.

- **Plan for repetition.** Be prepared for students to forget routines over time and to need to practice again. (Remember the frontal lobe discussed earlier in this section?) While eighth graders may forget what to do, they really do want to follow norms. Rather than presenting these as routines that *must* be followed, frame them in a way that shows how they foster the sense of belonging, significance, and fun in your class community.

See the appendix, p. 201, for more on Interactive Modeling.

Classroom Management and Responding to Misbehavior

"People usually learn something valuable *after* the first time they do it." I say this to my students every year. Then I go on to tell them a story about an innovation like the product WD-40—how "40" is the number of tries it took to get it right. In other words, mistakes are essential in an iterative learning process. In the classroom and for the rest of their life, students will find that there will be times when mistakes are made. By using logical consequences and managing our classroom in developmentally responsive ways, we can foster solutions-focused thinking rather than leaning on punishments.

Learning From Mistakes

Mistakes often trace back to a need. Eighth graders thrive on purposeful work, but their decision-making ability is still developing. Missing instructions, not paying attention, not prioritizing, forgetting homework (even if it's completed and in their backpack!), jumping ahead of themselves: all these behaviors are common at this age. From the start, we do everything we can to work with them to establish clear expectations and practice appropriate behaviors. The empathy that we model and practice daily helps our eighth graders view mistakes, along with the reasons behind them, as areas where they have room to grow.

When students' mistakes—or what I call "hiccups" or "speed bumps"—affect the classroom community, they need to be handled in a developmentally appropriate way that helps students learn. Teaching routines in a way that encourages students to be reflective, to slow down and take a step back before they move on, helps them develop lifelong strategies for self-discipline. The practice of using logical consequences aligns real-life expectations with our students' current environment, directly connecting the dots between the behavior and its consequence. And what better way to learn this lesson than in the safe space of their classroom community?

Loss of Privilege

One logical consequence for misbehavior is loss of privilege. I often describe this consequence to students with the phrase, "You abuse it, you lose it." My students learn that being in our classroom community is a privilege rather than a right. As members in our class with equal voice and agency, they are the ones who come up with the norms they will follow. When they forget or ignore those norms, it affects others. Loss of privilege is as simple as losing access to the privilege that was not used responsibly. For example, if students use computer research time to play games or look up kitten pictures (don't laugh—it's happened more than once!), they are asked to do the research independently with the prehistoric tool of books instead. If seemingly mature students suddenly turn the markers into lightsabers, they continue the work with pencils and/or must move seats to put some dis-

---

Rules Aren't Made to Be Broken!

What do you do if a classroom expectation or routine is never followed? Step back and look at the point where the expectation or routine breaks down to find the reason. Is it developmentally inappropriate for your class? Does it lack engagement or buy-in? Is it disconnected from their lives? Is it teacher driven? In the event that a routine is not working in your class, acknowledge to your students that it is ineffective and ask for their input. By recognizing your mistake, you give the classroom community an opportunity to design a better routine and model how mistakes help all of us discover a better way to do things.

tance between them. In a (very) brief conference, I remind students who have misbehaved that these consequences last for only a short time and explain how they can continue their learning in an alternate way. This consequence gives students time to reflect before regaining the privilege and using it in a way that's productive for everyone.

Final Word

Peer connection is everything at this age. When an eighth grade classroom is effectively managed, we can provide ample opportunities for students to interact with their peers, learn collaboratively, move, and yes, even be loud on occasion. In a classroom environment where it is safe to make mistakes, eighth graders can also learn the valuable lesson that they have the ability to overcome those mistakes. That's a life lesson that will stay with them for years to come.

Chapter 3
Positive Community

Overview

Picture again the developmentally responsive classroom we have been discussing. How does the teacher create an environment where students feel a strong sense of belonging and support each other as they exercise their own gifts and talents? What does this classroom space look like? First, respect is clearly evident between teacher and students and among the students. Students are not afraid to take risks, and the teacher uses language that is uplifting and supportive. You might see students consulting each other on a project, asking for help from those who demonstrate understanding, and supporting each other as they make their way through difficult activities. When misbehavior occurs, the teacher responds in a way that preserves students' dignity and the class expectations, viewing them as learning mistakes rather than intentional actions. When an individual student or small group experiences success, all students share in their triumph and celebrate alongside them.

How does one go about creating this environment? The development and maintenance of a positive community in a classroom is an essential step in creating the experience we have explored so far. While there are certain practical, defined ways to develop positive community, what results is far more than the sum of these parts—it's a learning space where all students feel a sense of safety, significance, and belonging.

Key Practices for Positive Community

There are certain key practices to help create a safe, predictable, joyful, and inclusive classroom where all students have a sense of belonging and significance. Teachers create a positive community in the following ways:

- **Teachers create the conditions for students to belong and be significant.** Each student brings their gifts to the classroom, and recognizing and encouraging these gifts helps the student feel significant among their classmates.

- **Teachers interact with students in a respectful manner.** We utilize positive teacher language in all that we do in order to preserve this positive environment and help students feel that they have the respect of their teacher and their classmates.

- **Teachers' approach to discipline is proactive.** Providing all students with clear expectations about their classroom experience can eliminate many behavior problems before they start. A classroom with these clear proactive expectations becomes a positive environment.

- **Teachers respond to misbehavior in ways that preserve the dignity of individual students and the class.** An environment with solid proactive procedures in place may show a reduction in unwanted behavior, but such behavior will still occasionally occur. One-on-one, quickly handled, and positive in nature, redirection can allow a student to get back on track without being humiliated or singled out. In other words, a student may be corrected without impacting their sense of belonging in the classroom.

- **Teachers provide opportunities to succeed that are equitable, fair, and just.** Your strong writers may feel success daily as they produce written products. Your mathematically gifted students may show their talents through computation. We can provide all of our students the opportunity to feel significant and experience success as they navigate their way through our school year. Each student brings their own skills and gifts, and we provide a foundation that includes those skills and gifts as part of the student's pathway to success.

Building the Foundation With a Daily Meeting

One way to get started is by implementing a Responsive Advisory Meeting to begin the day. Responsive Advisory Meeting is a core component of a middle school that is developmentally responsive to the unique strengths and needs of young adolescents. This daily event can provide students with the opportunity to build positive relationships with other students and with a specific adult in the building. Trust, respect, and cooperation are essential keys that can be developed through these meetings. Students begin to view their membership in the community as one with value, and they see the value in others, as well. The result is a classroom environment where our academic focus is partnered with the continuing respect and sense of belonging that all students feel while learning in a positive community.

See the appendix, p. 203, for more on Responsive Advisory Meetings.

Four Types of Teacher Language

One of the most powerful tools at your disposal when building a positive community is the one thing you probably do in your classroom more than anything else: talk! Teacher language is the professional use of words, phrases, tone, and pace we use in our daily interactions with students. Our language empowers all students to confidently engage with the curriculum content, learning activities, new ideas, and each other. It is the foundation of the classroom culture and is essential in our desire to build a positive community for learning and growth. We attempt to send messages of consistency, safety, and expectations for respectful communication and interactions among all students.

There are four distinct types of teacher language: envisioning, reinforcing, reminding, and redirecting. Throughout this chapter, we will explore the concept of teacher language more deeply by focusing on a different type in each section. We will explore reminding language in the sixth grade section, redirecting language in the seventh grade section, and reinforcing language in the eighth grade section. To begin to expand our understanding of teacher language, we will take a closer at envisioning language right now.

Envisioning Language

The statements and questions that help students create positive mental images of themselves are central to envisioning language. Envisioning language:

- **Inspires effort and persistence in our students.** Students can be inspired to see the positive outcomes of their efforts and will work hard when they see these outcomes as a reality. Reminding our middle school students of their achievements and helping them keep their goals in mind can encourage them to put forth their best effort.

- **Sets a positive tone for learning.** New learning can be difficult, but we can help students see what they can already accomplish and how those skills can be used to successfully complete new activities and assignments. This extends beyond academics and can be a help with developing their social and emotional proficiencies.

- **Builds a sense of belonging and community.** In order to be comfortable taking risks and working with others cooperatively, students must feel that they are important members of their learning community. This can encourage the whole class to value and practice cooperation, respect, and empathy.

Envisioning language is particularly important for middle schoolers as they begin to imagine what they are capable of, who they will become, and what they want to achieve. When students hear supportive, aspirational words from you, those messages will echo in their minds for years to come. They will repeat that sort of language in their self-talk and with their peers. Our words are powerful.

Proactive Discipline

A positive community is one in which students can feel safe making mistakes, including behavior missteps, and know that they will be met with a response that is respectful, preserves dignity, and starts from a place of understanding. Remember that discipline is teaching; we must help students learn how to behave in ways that result in their behavioral, social, and academic success. Our approach to teaching discipline with our students involves the implementation of both reactive and proactive discipline strategies. Reactive discipline strategies are intended to stop unwanted behavior in the moment, keep the focus on academics and learning, and help maintain safety. We discussed reactive strategies in Chapter 2. The primary goal of using proactive strategies—our focus in this chapter—is to create a safe, predictable, and joyful learning community where all students feel a sense of belonging and significance. We can establish this kind of community by creating, teaching, modeling, and reinforcing classroom procedures. These procedures can range from how to enter a classroom to how to calm down when stress levels rise. We will further explore these strategies in this chapter as we look at each grade level.

Ultimately, the goal of both proactive and reactive strategies is to move from a controlling approach to one that helps students develop self-control. Students need direct instruction in prosocial behaviors and opportunities to practice just as they do in any content area. The active, interactive, and appropriate learning experiences we design to teach discipline should be built on what we know about our students developmentally, personally, and culturally, which is why establishing a positive community is such a crucial step.

• • • • • • • • •

As you read this chapter, you will find strategies for building a classroom environment where students understand the expectations, are able to express themselves within the limits set by the teacher, and feel that success is within grasp each and every class period. As you consider how to best establish and maintain a positive community in your classroom, you will find relevant practices and approaches described in each grade-level section.

Grade

Once you get a sense of who your students are developmentally, and you think about effective classroom management, it's time to turn your attention toward building a positive community in your classroom. This is my passion point. It is important to me that my students feel safe in our classroom space and that they have a sense of belonging, significance, and fun. As an educator, especially at the middle school level, I believe that my job is to teach the whole child, not just course content. Of course, academic content is important, and it's taught for a reason, but there is something bigger at work in a sixth grade classroom. Students are learning who they are, how to interact and contribute to a larger community, and how to take risks, make mistakes, and try again. All of these aspirations are aided by the positive community that is created in your class.

High Expectations Lead to High Performance

In addition to being an important tool in effective management, teacher language also sets the tone for the community in your classroom. When speaking to sixth graders, it is important to use language that is direct and genuine—to say what you mean, and mean what you say. When you do this, students learn to trust you. With eleven- and twelve-year-olds who are looking for trusted adults, you want your language to say "You belong here." A statement like "Billie, that is not what a sixth grader does" tells Billie they don't belong; it isolates and removes them from the group. If a student is misbehaving, it is better to use redirecting language (more on that in the seventh grade section).

It is also important to convey faith in children's abilities and intentions. You may be familiar with the Pygmalion effect, in which high expectations lead to higher performance. Your expectations (whether high or low) impact students' beliefs, which impact their actions. Having high expectations of your students is more effective than having low expectations that you slowly raise. One reason, from my experience, is that students never know what is expected if you start low and then change the expectation. You're moving the finish line on someone in the middle of a race. Not knowing how to function in the space can lead a student to feel as if they don't belong there. Instead, the words you choose should tell students you believe in them and their ability to reach that finish line. Phrase your directions and guidance in a positive way, as students are more likely to repeat behaviors that are pointed out to them. For example, "Don't run in the hallway," framed in positive terms, would be "Walk in the hallway." "Don't forget to put your name, date, and class period at the top of the page" could become "Remind yourself of the paper headings protocol for social studies before you get started on your assignment."

> ### Using Positive Language
>
> Here are a few other examples to get you started:
>
> - "JoJo, you need to stop talking" becomes "JoJo, it's time to listen" (redirecting language).
> - "Why aren't your materials out?" becomes "Pencils and books out" (reminding language).
> - "Do not disrespect the guest teacher" becomes "Remember to show respect to the guest teacher" (reminding language).

Using Silence Skillfully

Another important piece of teacher language, although it may feel counterintuitive, is to use silence skillfully. Consider the following scenario. In a social studies lesson, I ask my students, "In what year was the Declaration of Independence written?" Addison answers, "It was written in 1776." Some educators might then repeat, "Right, 1776." Instead, I give a nod of affirmation and move on. If the room is noisy and I'm concerned others did not hear Addison, then I might say, "Addison, amplify." This quick word signals that I want Addison to repeat the words a little louder. The student voice is still the one being heard by classmates. Teacher silence can allow student voices to be more prominent and help develop independence among students, rather than fostering teacher dependence. Students can be intrinsically motivated by the feeling they get from being brave and sharing with the class. Conversely, they may feel discouraged when the teacher repeats what they've said, taking away their agency and voice in the space. Silence can also give students the chance to process new information and form their own thoughts and opinions.

Reminding Language

As you get to know the eleven- and twelve-year-olds in front of you, their bold yet tentative nature and their attempts to test the limits of the classroom will lead you to use positive teacher language as a proactive discipline strategy. I sometimes refer to sixth grade as the kindergarten of secondary education. It's the point at which students are starting a new chapter in which many of the things they knew about school are different. They are working with more teachers, more classes, and a new schedule, all while managing those raging hormones. In sixth grade, reminding language can be particularly beneficial.

Reminding language helps our students to remember the expectations that we have established and helps them to practice responsibility and control. For example, before heading to the library, you might ask your class, "What classroom expectations are especially important in the library?" As students get ready to complete some independent practice, you might say, "Think about how we completed the sample exercise together as you get started." In both of these examples, students are led to refer back either to classroom expectations or to your routines and procedures, allowing them to set the positive mental image of what they should be doing. There will also be times when you will need to use redirecting or reinforcing language with your students. You'll find more information on these two types of teacher language in the seventh and eighth grade sections. Understanding how to use positive teacher language is a career-long journey, but practicing can start immediately.

In order to benefit most from reminding language, students need to know what the expectations are. In Chapter 2, we talked about effective management as it relates to displaying your classroom expectations (again, I prefer "expectations" to "rules") prominently in your classroom. A suggestion for how to create those expectations was also shared. So now that you've established the expectations, how do you invest students in following them, and why is this important? When students are invested in the rules, they care about how the class operates. They learn how the contributions of the individuals can impact the success of the whole. Students are also more likely to feel that sense of belonging when they know how the room operates, which increases their confidence, allows others to get to know them, and builds their sense of significance. In sixth grade, our students become increasingly loyal to their classmates and peers, and they seem to have a positive energy toward the group. Using these innate characteristics to our advantage, this desire for and loyalty toward community can help invest students in the classroom expectations.

Keeping the Rules Alive

There are a few other ways to invest students in the rules or expectations of your classroom. Connecting students' individual goals to classroom rules lets students see how following these expectations helps everyone reach their goals. Many teachers create a list of rules, go over them on the first day of school, and maybe stick them on a poster in the back of the room to never be spoken of again. Rather than follow that path, keep the rules alive for your students. Reference them regularly, with questions like "Which of our class expectations will be helpful for us during our project today?" Or, when students are beginning a test, you might ask, "During our test today, which of our class expectations will we want to pay particular attention to?"

It is also helpful to go over the expectations in a bit more depth, a refresher course if you

Creating Classroom Rules

The expectations for my classes typically include some combination of the following elements: respect yourself, respect others, respect our classroom environment. Respecting the classroom environment can apply to the atmosphere in the room, the learning that happens, and the materials. The universal nature of these expectations allows us to stay focused on the tasks at hand without getting bogged down by narrowly worded rules.

will, after holiday breaks or at the start of a new term. Doing so reestablishes the culture of support and community. To maintain consistency, the expectations in my classes do not change throughout the year. However, if there is a need to address a pattern of behavior or a concern that arises, you can use the existing classroom expectations to address it. For example, imagine your classroom expectations at the beginning of the year include respecting others and yourself. But after a couple of months, you notice students are mistreating books in the classroom library or not taking care of classroom materials. Then you might need to add an expectation like "respect materials." To invest students in the rules, and still have them be a part of this process, you could take some time out of class to address the concern and ask what sort of guideline or expectation might help everyone to remember to take care of these materials. Keeping rules or expectations universal in nature allows them to fit many scenarios.

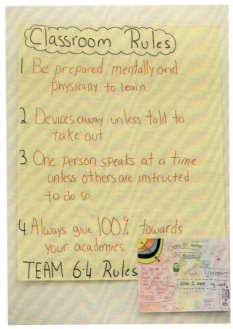 

The First Day of School

Your teacher language and classroom expectations set the tone for the class beginning on the first day of school, and the same is true for establishing a positive community. I do my best to stand at the door at the beginning of each class hour and greet students as they enter the classroom. (As soon as I've learned their names, I greet them by name.) Providing this greeting starts a student's time in your room feeling like the teacher knows and cares about them, and are glad they are there. Consider this experience of a sixth grader on the first day of school:

> Walking toward their social studies classroom, Taylor approaches the teacher at the doorway. The teacher greets them with a smile, asks their name, and says, "Welcome, Taylor. Find a seat at the yellow table and read the message on the board." Taylor enters the space knowing where to go, settles into their seat, and looks at the screen, which reads "Welcome, historians! I'm glad you are here. While you wait for class to start, think of one word that describes how you are feeling today. Be prepared to share." The teacher then enters the class, introduces themself, and has students turn to the person sitting next to them to share their name and their one word.

In these first few minutes, the teacher has shown the students they are valued; established an academic tone with the envisioning language of "Welcome, historians!"; given students a peer in the room whose name they know; and given each student the opportunity to make a connection about how they are feeling on the first day.

> **Quick Tip**
> At the start of the year, sharing should be safe. Students haven't built up trust yet with classmates, so sharing shouldn't be too personal or too long.

Interactive Learning

If all of that can happen in five minutes, imagine the community that can be built when interactive learning structures or brain breaks are used daily and students are encouraged to get to know one another.

Interactive learning structures often lend themselves to small-group work. Remember, though, that while small groups are an excellent tool, sixth graders can often be irresponsible in small groups. Take time at the start of your school year to set up routines and expectations around small-group work. Having a specific role to fill (facilitator, materials manager, reporter, recorder) can support students in fulfilling these expectations. These small-group roles are easily adaptable to hybrid, socially distanced, or tech-inclusive learning formats.

Final Word

One of my colleagues shared a simple strategy that goes a long way toward letting students know the classroom is a space for them and aiding in building community. They put up a calendar in an easily accessible space in the classroom. Near the first of the month, they invite students to add their birthdays, performances, sports games and tournaments, and things they are proud of and want their class and teacher to know about.

Students can also be invited to add holidays they celebrate to the calendar, and to share with the class how they celebrate them. This opportunity for sharing recognizes the diverse cultures in the room and opens up class dialogue, both of which contribute to a positive classroom community.

Grade

A few years ago, I had students bring in a piece of wisdom to share with the class. This could be in the form of an anecdote, a personal motto, or good advice they had received from someone important in their life. One student shared a simple adage: "The day you plant the seeds is not the day you eat the fruit." I think about this quote often, and I even have a handwritten copy of it on my desk. It reminds me that though there will be many times that it doesn't seem like I'm getting through to my seventh graders, I know that it is a worthy investment to continue to plant and nurture those seeds.

This is an especially important reminder to us as we think about how we can build a positive community in our seventh grade classrooms. There will be days when it feels like connections are really being forged and that students are learning and valuing empathy, cooperation, and kindness. Then there will be days when it seems like the students don't remember those lessons at all. Think back to what we covered in Chapter 1; this is a time of intense social shifting, physical change, and increased academic pressure. These twelve- and thirteen-year-olds are traversing a world where they are disengaging from their parents and teachers but are still not fully equipped to navigate the unpredictable social world of their peer group. While their instinct might be to pull away, we know this is a critical time for the adults in their lives to be a safe and supportive presence.

Finding Common Ground

So how can you build a community when seventh graders' developmental instinct is to pull apart? While building a positive community should be a part of everything we do in school, a practical place to start, as mentioned in the overview for this chapter, is with Responsive Advisory Meeting. Some schools may have this time built into their schedules, while others may not. For those who do have time set aside for the purpose of advisory, it's a great opportunity to start off the school year with positive community-building activities. For our seventh graders, highly structured "get to know me, get to know you" activities are a wonderful way to help students

See the appendix, p. 203, for more on Responsive Advisory Meetings.

begin to forge relationships with one another. For example, you might have students complete a fill-in-the-blank paragraph to provide some basic information about themselves, create individual and group collages, or play a game of All Many Few. Activities that have lots of structure and involve a task for them to complete help support our socially insecure seventh graders. The end result has the benefit of students sharing a bit of themselves with their classmates while also making connections to others.

> **All Many Few**
> This is a game where students write down three statements: something they think everyone in the room has in common, many people in the room have in common, and few people in the room have in common with themselves. For example, "I'm a Tiger [or other school mascot]," "I have moved at least once," and "I love mayo on my french fries."

Students who feel like valued members of the group are more likely to be engaged learners, cooperate with their peers, and enjoy their time spent in class. In the case that you do not have a designated advisory time it is still a worthwhile investment to take a short time out of class every few weeks for these types of community-building activities.

I've had the most success with building community in a seventh grade classroom around a common interest or passion project. One year, I had a class that was really into time-lapse cooking videos. Whenever we had a few minutes at the end of class, they would all happily watch a compilation of cookie recipes or cake decorating tips. They would keep a running commentary throughout the whole video and would critique the various treats as though they were commentators on a sports broadcasting program. It became their "thing," so much so that at the end of the semester, we hosted a party where they could bring in their own treats to share with the class. They even brought plates of goodies to their teachers!

Other years, I've had groups that were more artistic types, and their "thing" was designing and decorating the bulletin board by our classroom door. Another group decided they wanted a class pet. I told them they could have a pet rock, and much to my surprise, they brought in a pet rock, named it

"Juicy" (still not entirely sure why) and it became something they happily dedicated their time and energy to every morning during homeroom.

While not every class will have a "thing," and not every "thing" will come along right at the beginning of the school year, it can be such a powerful way to build a positive community in your classroom because it connects a group of kids who otherwise are at a stage of their development where they are fracturing from one another. Research has shown time and again that shared experiences offer deep and long-lasting psychological benefits; at a time when students are going through the roller-coaster ride that is seventh grade, these experiences provide something fun and unifying. It requires some flexibility on our part and a willingness to get to know our students. For example, with the group that loved to watch baking videos, I would arrange our class time so that our lesson could be wrapped up about five minutes before the bell rang, but students also knew that they had to be on track so that we would have the time to watch. With my bulletin board artists, I provided the basic materials and they would spend time during homeroom planning and preparing their various pieces. One important note: for each of these groups of kids, their fun community activity was serious business to them! When I took time to treat their interests with equal seriousness and respect, it resulted in intrinsic motivation for these students to be active and engaged members of the class. A small investment on my part paid great dividends in building positive classroom culture.

Ending Each Day With Purpose

Often, the most hectic part of our day is the very end; the last five minutes before the end of class or the end of school can feel frantic, chaotic, and, with middle schoolers, loud! Can you imagine if we could end the day calmly and joyfully? I find closing circle to be a valuable practice with my students, especially my seventh graders. Closing circle is a short, whole-group activity aimed at ending the class period or school day on a positive note.

It took time to get the seventh graders to buy into the idea because it is outside of the normal experience of bell to bell, but toward the end of the first semester, it became a practice that students really looked forward to each day. For example, the very first closing circle I do with students is Ball Toss, where each member of the group says a classmate's name and tosses them the ball until everyone has had their name called. Then we go in reverse! It's a great way for everyone to begin to learn their classmates' names. As the year progresses, I introduce a variety of games, challenges, quick sharing topics ("something you were proud of today," "your favorite flavor of ice cream"), and open-ended questions for discussions. Ending the day on a positive note builds community and helps students refocus, reflect, and prepare for the next class or rest of their day.

I've implemented closing circle in different ways with my classes; some years, it's been the last period of the day (we have a rotation schedule that makes this work); in other years, I've only done closing circles on a specific day of the week. It can be a big ask to sacrifice five minutes of valuable class time, but I treat this as an important part of our class, and so do students. On days they know they will have a closing circle, we also know that we have to prioritize staying on task so we can have time for it. It's an excellent intrinsic motivator and opportunity to build social and emotional skills with the added bonus of strengthening our classroom community.

Developing Group Identity

For those of us who don't see our students every day, building a positive community can be challenging. Seventh graders like to be both unique and part of a group; while this is seemingly contradictory, one idea is to

embrace both of these desires with class names. This can be something you come up with, something that gives them choice, or something they come up with entirely on their own. Having a class name can make groups feel like they're special—distinct from the other groups you teach. It can also be a fun way to reflect their personalities (every group has one!), and it's an opportunity to encourage students to create positive mental images of themselves. (See the overview to this chapter for more on envisioning language.) For example, I have a colleague who does this with his students in the first few weeks of school. He's had a group call themselves "The Big Brains"; another group was "The Tractor Tims." You might ascribe a specific color, food, or animal to a group—a great tip for organizing your lesson plans as well as giving your groups a sense of identity! Think of how it might be thematic as well; an art teacher could have groups represented by art movements, while PE classes can be identified by different types of sporting events.

Investing Students in the Rules

Another important way to deepen students' connection to each other is by investing them in the classroom rules. I find that seventh graders often need more guidance on this, as twelve- and thirteen-year-olds sometimes seem like their default settings are "It's all about me" and "Whatever adults say must be wrong." What we want them to know is that the rules are in place not to control them, but to help them accomplish their goals and be valued members of the group. Remember—we're planting seeds!

I start with my three class rules ("Be responsible," "Be respectful," and "Be ready"), and each class comes up with ways they will demonstrate each rule. Then, throughout the year, we revisit our class expectations with prompts like these:

- "What does 'ready' look like when we're about to take a test or quiz?"
- "Make a list of all the things we are responsible for to make sure we complete this project on time."
- "How can we show a speaker respect when they're giving their presentation?"

I find that it's a good idea to have the answers I expect in mind when facilitating these discussions with your students; this helps me to make sure they've hit all the points I want them to note.

Clear and Explicit Expectations

When thinking about being proactive in our discipline practice, what we're really asking is how we can set students up for behavioral success. With all middle school students, it's beneficial to have clear and explicit expectations in place. I find this especially relevant with seventh graders; the clearer and narrower our parameters are with them, the less room there is for them to make a behavior mistake. This is demonstrated in the example of moving around in the hallways. Twelve- and thirteen-year-olds are very creative; if our rule is "Don't run," then they'll come up with plenty of ideas that do not involve running: skipping, power walking, cartwheeling, shoving, dancing . . . all of these are technically not running! Instead, simply telling our students that their one and only option is to walk makes this much easier for us to monitor and much clearer for them to follow. This same principle extends into everything else a seventh grader might do: trash goes in the trash can, tuck in your chair whenever you're not in it, say "please" and "thank you" when asking a classmate for a favor or request. Kids feel safe when they know what is expected, and they are more likely to be engaged with the learning, too. This simple, proactive practice helps reduce the amount of negotiation some students will engage in or time you need to spend explaining what to do—and leaves more room for learning and fun.

Teacher Language

A colleague of mine shared with me a lovely analogy that she had been taught for thinking about teacher language: "Our words are the water students swim in and the air they breathe." When I think of my words in this way, it helps me to understand their power, and I'm motivated to not "pollute" the classroom environment. We want our language to be direct and genuine, convey faith in our students' abilities, focus on actions, be brief and focused, and skillfully use silence. With these basic principles in place, our language will create an environment in which children can grow and thrive.

In the seventh grade classroom, we should be extra conscious of the developmental stage students are in; they can be sensitive to our words, especially in how those words are identity forming. Again, let's return to the concept of envisioning language. A class labeled as a "bad class" will be more likely to engage in negative and undesirable behaviors. Talking to that same class about actions that do not align with our class agreements or expectations, along with conveying the belief that they can and will do better, is a much more effective way of addressing problems. We should also remember that we are constantly modeling adult behavior to students; seventh graders have an increasing desire to be perceived as "mature," "adult," or "grown-up," but the models they choose for this kind of behavior are not always conducive to the classroom. We can teach prosocial behaviors by the way we act and interact with our students, especially in our choice of language.

Redirecting Language

In our classrooms, we can consciously use reminding language (see the sixth grade section), reinforcing language (see the eighth grade section), and redirecting language to build positive communities. Remember the example with "not running" in hallways? I find that I most often use redirecting language with my seventh grade classes. The key characteristics of redirecting language are as follows:

- **It is short and specific.** Redirecting statements avoid elaboration and get straight to the desired behavior or action.

- **It provides clear instructions.** With clear instructions, students understand exactly what is expected of them at that moment. This is bolstered even more when the instructions are consistent, reviewed at the beginning of the class or lesson, and are accessible via a visual aid.

- **It is said in the moment.** When we respond immediately to a situation, it helps students to quickly get back on track. We want to use redirecting language when something is about to go awry or off track; this helps students to make the appropriate adjustments before something more problematic occurs.

- **It includes names.** As often as we can, we want to attach a name to our redirecting language by addressing the child directly. This both acknowledges the child and makes it clear to whom the instruction is being directed.

Here are some examples of how you might use redirecting language in your own interactions with students:

Instead of . . .	Try . . .
"Look at the mess you're making!"	"Scissors are only for cutting paper for our project. If you're done, return them to the box."
"You're being too loud!"	"Silence your voices while you're in the library."
"Don't dribble your basketball."	"When you're in line, the basketball stays in your hands."
"You're being mean to your classmates."	"We speak to each other in a kind and respectful way only."

The effectiveness of redirecting language lies in the fact that it doesn't allow for choice or argument; there is only one option, which aligns with our classroom rules and expectations. We're telling students what to do instead of what not to do. It is also presented to students without judgment or a lecture on their current actions. Instead, it directs them toward the behaviors they are expected to be using at that moment. Of course, if their actions or behaviors are harmful, beyond redirection, or the redirection is disregarded, we should consider using logical consequences. (See Chapter 2.)

Final Word

There are so many aspects of seventh graders' lives and learning that we can influence by building a positive classroom community and culture. As teachers, we must think about the ways in which students know and get to be known by their classmates, how they make connections with one another, the common experiences they will share, and the language we use to build these positive mental images and identities. It's a tall order for teachers, on top of delivering curriculum! While there are times when I would certainly rather just get through the material, I know that it is vitally important for seventh graders that these important social and emotional skills are taught and modeled. Taking time to do so, even if it's just five minutes at the beginning or end of class, is a worthy investment.

Grade

Humans do what they've been taught. Several years ago, I saw a new teacher carrying a big bag of popcorn across the campus. I asked her about it and she told me, "The class filled their marble jar, so they're getting a popcorn party!" I thought to myself, "Huh, that's an approach I haven't seen for a while." I assumed new teachers' practices had evolved and that they are now taught that while extrinsic reward systems may be effective in the short term, they tend to fail in long-term behavioral impact. I mentioned these thoughts to my principal, and she wisely said, "It depends on who taught them." The same is true for your students.

There is such a developmental and social shift at the eighth grade age that teachers often face the challenge of building an equitable class community from the ground up. As developmentally responsive educators, we want to always start with the things most important at this age: peer relations (maintaining connections with each other) and agency (student ownership of their school experience).

At the beginning of the year, eighth graders feel a keen (most of the time!) social and emotional awareness, making them ripe for opportunities to model positive behavior for and share connections with other students. On the other hand, there are times when they are just trying to navigate the pressure to learn where they fit in. During this time of uncertainty, it's essential to cultivate students' self-awareness and potential, to build a place where our students know they have significance, to create the community to provide that important security, and—let's face it—give them one less thing they have to figure out and remember. That's exactly why this is the perfect time to establish predictable routines, consistent support, and regular opportunities to contribute.

In previous chapters, we've talked about the ways our eighth graders can look like adults, yet still need our support and boundaries. They need to feel seen and heard. Positive community has three areas of focus:

1. **Class structure.** We strive to create both a space and a way of learning that are student driven and where each student has an equal voice.

2. **Academics.** Meaningful academic content is a timely blend of must-teach standards and the particular interests of our students (more on this in Chapter 4).

3. **Discipline.** Once students see the impact of the community, they are invested in designing structures and norms to keep it vibrant and successful.

Investing Students in the Rules

In Chapter 1, we considered the phrase "Go slow so you can go fast." In the case of creating a classroom community, we can frame this for our students as a gift of time. Spending a week (or more!) at the beginning of the year working with your students to create a custom class structure—and the rules and expectations to maintain that structure—will support collaborative work later. As teachers of eighth graders, there are some developmental aspects to keep in mind. For instance, students this age are quick to argue about everything, especially rules they feel are unfair or pointless. To establish an environment of mutual respect from day one, it's a good idea to spend a session or two on an initial whole-class brainstorm to develop suggestions for rules or norms the students need to create a

> ### Connect Back to Why
> The "why" of what they are learning is an essential hook for our students. A priority for students this age is to understand the question "What does this have to do with me?" As developmentally responsive teachers, we work from the minute we meet our students to learn about them. This gives us the added bonus that when students ask, "What does this have to do with me?" the answer—the "why"—is custom-tailored to what we know about our students. I call this "stealth teaching"; we are helping them meet their goals, and they don't even know it!

place where they can be their best learning and collaborative selves. Negotiation and compromise are embedded as we work to find common ground. My goal with this activity is less *me*, more *we*. You will read the room and learn the needs of your class as you do this with each section, class, or period. It's perfectly appropriate to have a different brainstorm session with each class and either combine the rules into one list or keep them separate. With this, they will see their opinion matters.

I do this brainstorm process with sticky notes—bright, colorful ones we write on with skinny markers. Students at this age respond well to visual learning tools like this (and it's fun!). To begin, I place a pile of sticky notes and markers on collaborative work spaces and provide the following instructions:

Reflect, imagine, or design your ideal learning community.

- What elements are present?
- What do you need to be successful?"

I'll model with a relevant example, such as "Time to talk with my friends," and then write it on a whiteboard or alternate display area. Ideas usually start slowly, with a trickle of contributions, before the snowball starts rolling down the hill. I give students five minutes or so (this limit tends to focus them) to record their ideas and put them on the board. After this time, we look at the contributions and read as many as possible out loud before we start to group them. I purposefully talk through my thinking as I model this categorization to support their future learning. Once we come up with four or five

Class Meetings

The overarching goal of a developmentally responsive teacher is to address both the academic and the social and emotional competencies of our students. Once the community norms are established, we can start applying them in settings such as class meetings. This approach helps students to practice real-world skills like clear communication, idea and behavior ownership, and independent thinking, and also builds on their need for peer connections. Class meetings capitalize on both the agency students need to experience and the compromise and give-and-take they need to be exposed to in order to better navigate high school and beyond.

common categories (I call them norms, although you can use any label that works for you), I rephrase the idea to honor its intent, for example, "It looks like several class members mentioned the need for open-minded listening. How does 'Maintain open mind with others' sound to you? Thumbs-up or thumbs-down? Can everyone live with that norm? No? That's okay. How can we say it better?" I work to keep the process quick, respectful, efficient, and always, *always* let them know they are heard. It's an easy way to model compromise, invest students in their classroom, and ensure that everyone's contribution is honored.

Reinforcing Language

A specific, targeted practice that really pulls a developmentally responsive classroom together is teacher language. I think of it as the foundation on which everything is built. When I was being observed one time, the mentor noted, "I didn't hear you correct a student at all." I answered truthfully, "Rather than being the perfect teacher, I work hard to notice when students demonstrate the norms *they* created. It circumvents so many problems." This simple shift in outlook supports the growth of many positive behaviors and illustrates how agency and ownership come together for our students.

In the chapter overview, you learned about the four types of teacher language: envisioning, reinforcing, reminding, and redirecting. In my practice, I lean on reinforcing language more than any other type to create a strong community. Some teachers call the concept behind this practice "getting caught being good," but I'll transparently admit I avoid labels like "good" and "bad." Instead, I work on recognizing room to grow. Reinforcing language shows what is working and uses specific language to elevate and continue the behavior. Effective reinforcing language includes these key elements:

- **It focuses on a specific and concrete description of the behavior.** Focus students' attention on their replicable actions rather than on your personal approval. This makes it easy for them to understand exactly what they did, and what to do again, for the right reasons.

- **It is applied equitably with all students.** Everyone deserves to be recognized for something—big or small. Students are unique, and the relationships you've built early on with your students will tell you exactly how to best support them.

- **It is delivered sincerely.** Remember how students this age are well attuned to the emotions of others? Any insincerity they sense will break important trust between you. It's essential in all cases—especially when using teacher language—that we mean what we say and say what we mean.

- **It recognizes individual behavior privately, and demonstrations of group norms publicly.** Students dislike hearing comments—either positive or negative—applicable to one person being directed to all. By putting the spotlight on one of them, you are reminding the rest what they are not doing or potentially making an individual feel uncomfortable. Not a good feeling for anyone. Relatedly, when many students demonstrate an expected behavior, group recognition supports the collective effort.

So what does this look like in practice? These common scenarios show how reinforcing language is commonly used in middle school classrooms:

Situation	Reinforcing Language
Class discussion	"Nicholas, you really wanted to say something and patiently stopped yourself. That's an example of 'One person talks at a time.'"
Passing period	"I noticed everyone steered around Daria as she kneeled to tie her shoe. That really respects our rule to keep everyone safe."
Collecting materials	"Donovan, you remembered to put the scissors and markers back in their place. That's a considerate way to support everyone's learning."
Collaborative group projects	"I'm hearing so much productive noise . . . and seeing lots of give-and-take in the conversations!"

Final Word

One of the best effects of using reinforcing language is how its positive impact spreads throughout the class community. Once each student feels how your supportive comments recognize their constructive behaviors, they often begin to speak to each other in optimistic ways. As a result, this spreading positive impact becomes the gift that keeps on giving, helping to create the belonging, significance, and fun we always envisioned!

Chapter 4
Engaging Academics

Overview

Over the last few chapters, we have focused on how a responsive, effective, and positive classroom looks and feels to both teacher and students. We have discussed the teacher's flexibility, the students' level of comfort, and the mutual respect between teacher and students. Perhaps those descriptions made teaching seem effortless and easy, but it's quite the opposite: there is much that happens behind the scenes to make meaningful learning happen. Most of what we have discussed requires significant forethought and planning on the part of the individual teacher, along with the partnership of the entire teaching staff. While this important aspect of teaching doesn't usually happen when students are in the classroom and often goes unobserved, its impact is unmistakable.

In this chapter, we'll consider the daily planning that goes into making the joyful classroom a reality. Everything we have discussed so far—getting to know students developmentally, managing the classroom effectively so all students are seen and supported, and building positive learning communities—provides the framework for designing academics that engage and challenge all learners. Infusing our lessons with what we know about our students individually, culturally, and developmentally makes for deeper learning, strengthens our relationships with our students, and sparks academic connections that will serve our students long after their time in our class has ended.

The Natural Learning Cycle

As we consider how to provide engaging academic experiences for all students, we first need to make sure learning is pedagogically sound, supported by a lesson design that leverages the natural learning cycle. The most meaningful learning happens when our brains engage in an iterative cycle of learning grounded in a sense of purpose. If we approach our own teaching and our students' learning from the foundation of this brain-based approach, we can be sure that deep and effective learning can take place.

There are three phases to the natural learning cycle. It begins when we generate *ideas and goals*. These are like the hopes and dreams we may envision at the beginning of the school year. We help students create meaningful goals grounded in both the curriculum and their personal interests.

After ideas and goals are generated, we progress through *active exploration*, *experimentation*, and *problem-solving*. In this second phase, students are given academic choices which, along with check-ins and support, can help them connect their daily work to their long-term learning goals.

Finally, we guide students through the process of *reflecting* on their experiences. How have the work and learning they have done connected to their original ideas and goals? What worked, and what didn't work? We then guide students to return to generate new goals and ideas for the next cycle of learning.

Meaningful Lesson Design

In order for students to engage in the natural learning cycle during our classes, we must introduce content and skills through purposeful and meaningful lessons designed around our curricular objectives. Utilizing a three-part lesson design loosely connected to the stages of the natural learning cycle can motivate students to engage fully in their learning. As you implement each of these three stages of an engaging lesson, consider what the students are wondering and how your teaching can lay the groundwork for their learning.

- **Opening: What will I learn? Why does it matter?** Middle school students need to know what they are doing, and why. Why is the class reading a specific piece of literature? Why are they focused on the parts of speech or on a spelling list? Once students know the purpose behind what they are studying, they are better able to make a personal connection to the material because they will see why it is important to them.

- **Body: How do I learn this? What else do I need to know?** Student engagement is the focus during this part of the lesson. Here, students move beyond watching and listening and begin to practice by digging into their lessons, trying out new concepts, and researching topics that interest them. The teacher's role at this time is to observe students and coach if needed.

- **Closing: What did I learn? How did I learn it? What can I do next time?** The method we use to end a lesson is just as important as how we begin. Through reflection, all students can gain a stronger understanding of both the material learned and the method for learning it. Also, achieving a sense of closure allows students to move on cleanly from the lesson to other academic or social events.

Active Teaching

We can deepen the natural learning cycle and amplify students' innate curiosity by meeting their questions, whether implicit or explicit, with active teaching. This strategy brings together students' developmental strengths, their need for fun and social interaction, and a clear, goal-oriented, demonstrable approach to attaining learning objectives. Consider each of these three phases of active teaching as responses to the hypothetical student questions posed above in the three parts of a lesson:

- **Teacher instructs and models.** Use a combination of words and images to help students store new learning. Instruction is delivered using words and nonlinguistic representations to create mental images that aid in learning.

- **Students collaborate.** Students discuss new learning in small groups or with a partner while the teacher facilitates. Students have opportunities to analyze what you as their teacher have modeled, giving them a chance to work on their observation skills and see their capabilities as members of the academic community.

- **Teacher facilitates reflection.** Reflection helps students become more aware of how they learn. This phase is more than simply recounting or restating what students have done. When students understand what strategies work for them, they can adapt the strategies and apply them to other learning situations.

Strategies for Meaningful Learning

Active teaching and engaging lesson design are useful strategies for supporting meaningful learning in middle school classrooms. To promote this high level of academic exploration, teachers embolden students to explore, experiment, and examine new ideas and skills independently and with classmates. Using effective questioning techniques, posing a variety of questions, and encouraging student questions are all crucial tools in the active teacher's toolbox. Setting high expectations for all students and offering appropriately challenging lessons and experiences are part of engaging students in their own learning.

Active teaching and engaging lesson design have those adjectives for a reason: teachers are always busy when using these strategies. Even when students may be collaborating or working independently, teachers are monitoring their progress to make decisions about learning, to provide high-quality feedback, and to reinforce efforts or clear up confusion. Observing students is what allows us to tailor instruction and support to meet the needs of individual students and groups.

Culturally Relevant and Responsive Teaching

Intentionally designing academic lessons to engage and motivate students also creates an important opportunity for us to be culturally relevant and

responsive. In earlier chapters, we discussed the importance of getting to know our students individually, developmentally, and culturally to build a positive community and be responsive in our teaching. For instance, lessons that allow students to share about themselves and learn about each other can help to build a positive classroom community and healthy connections among students. Students may be able to build more trusting relationships among their peers as they practice the social and emotional skills of respect, empathy, and clarity in all their interactions, and contribute to a classroom environment grounded in those qualities.

By applying these same ideas to our teaching practice, we can also create an environment where academic activities build on our knowledge of students' individual cultures, contribute to the building of trust among peers, and leverage learning styles and tools from different cultures.

• • • • • • • • •

Throughout this chapter, you will see suggestions for ways to make lessons social and energized with interactive learning structures, encourage student voice and agency in learning, and incorporate your knowledge of your students and what they need. No matter what grade you teach, you will find relevant practices and approaches described in each grade-level section. You can go directly to the section for the grade level you teach, or you can read the entire chapter, including the sixth, seventh, and eighth grade sections. Each grade-level section is different and focuses on a slightly different aspect of engaging academics for middle schoolers. The sixth grade section delves more deeply into lesson design, while the seventh grade section offers suggestions for providing the structure and safety students need to effectively explore and take risks in their learning. The eighth grade section discusses how project-based learning and culturally responsive teaching are important tools for building student voice and activism.

All of the approaches shared in this chapter help us support our students in learning the strategies, skills, and content that will serve them well in and out of the classroom. After all, how we teach is as important as what we teach.

Grade

When I think back to sitting in a classroom as a middle school student, there are two different scenarios that I clearly remember. The first is a math teacher who would sit next to the overhead projector for the entire class and do example problems, and then tell us to complete the even-numbered questions for that section. The other scenario was a US Senate simulation in social studies. Each student was assigned a senator, and we wrote laws, met in committees, and voted on whether or not to pass new laws so they could be sent to the president (a teacher in a different classroom) for signature or veto. I used to dread going to math class but was often excited to head to social studies. As I reflect on these two different classroom experiences, I can see where the interaction with material in social studies helped draw me in and made me feel like a part of the learning. In math class, however, I was sitting, getting, and practicing, but not firing up my brain to really engage in the work.

When students are active participants in their learning, they are more likely to be engaged. When they are engaged, they have room to discover their passions and develop new skills. The question is, how do we create those engaging academic opportunities for all of our students?

Lesson Design

As you think about creating engaging academics for your students, the first thing to focus on is lesson design. There are many different templates, models, and formats for designing your lessons. One format you may choose to use is as follows:

- **Anticipatory set.** Introduce something short at the start of a lesson to grab students' attention and activate prior knowledge. This may look like doing a short warm-up activity, asking a thought-provoking question, or sharing a KWL chart.

- **Learning objective.** Outlines the goal for students to achieve by the end of a lesson.

- **Active teaching.** This is different from direct instruction, when students are sitting in a seat and getting information lecture-style. As discussed in the overview to this chapter, active teaching is made up of three phases:
    - **Teacher instructs and models.** Examples include graphic organizers, videos, kinesthetic activities, and visuals.
    - **Students collaborate.** Examples include partner shares, small-group work, and discovery. This is a great opportunity for students to practice communication skills and social and emotional learning skills. Small-group learning is also a way to help meet the developmental needs of your students, who desire the time to interact with their peers, build relationships, and cooperate.
    - **Teacher facilitates reflection.** Examples include reflection questions, journal prompts, or structured discussions that connect to the learning objective.
- **Teacher-directed student practice.** Students are given a chance to practice the content they have just learned, while the teacher offers feedback through formative assessment that is focused on mastering a skill versus getting a certain score.
- **Independent practice.** Students are able to complete work on their own, which helps to solidify new learning as they engage with the content and practice new skills.
- **Closure.** This wraps up the learning and helps students to organize the information in their minds.

> **Quick Tip**
>
> I find that sometimes it can take me several days to work through these parts, but each day I still start with something anticipatory, and end with a closure of some kind.

With this structure in mind, it's time to get to work. I begin with a look at the content standards and think about how students will demonstrate understanding, starting with envisioning what the end goal is. You may find in your content area that a standard takes days or even weeks to teach, so you will need to find natural breaks in the content.

Anticipatory Set

When you think of structuring a daily lesson, start with an anticipatory set, as discussed in the previous section. Sixth graders, for the most part, enjoy learning but are wary of making mistakes. An anticipatory set gives you an opportunity to hook the students on your content or to engage in your community. You might ask an open-ended question about the subject or answer some questions on an anticipation guide. If you teach in a school with one-to-one devices, consider having students fill out an online form once a week during this time. A survey gives students a chance to check in with you in a low-stakes yet personal way. Questions might include:

- How did you sleep last night? (1–5 scale)
- How are things outside of school? (1–5 scale)
- Is there anything you'd like your teacher to know? (short answer)

You can also ask content-related questions, like:

- What is a cell?
- In this math problem, what step is first?
- What is the Constitution?

For me, this weekly survey offers a small glimpse into how my students are doing outside of school. It's also a safe way for students to share information with teachers.

Learning Objective

After this, it's time to share the learning objective. Your school may require language and content objectives to be posted or may not require formal objectives at all. Regardless, it is still a good idea to start a lesson by telling students what the goal is. Explain what they should be able to do at the end of the lesson (or after a series of days spent on the topic) to give them a target to aim for. Middle school students, and especially sixth graders, feel more comfortable and more able to engage when they understand the context and what is expected of them. It helps you and them if you are clear about these parameters right away.

Active Teaching

With the goal in sight, your next step is the instructional part of the lesson. Here is the shift from traditional direct teaching, where a teacher does most of the work by standing and lecturing, to active teaching, where students are more involved in exploring and experimenting and the teacher is the facilitator. You'll start with teaching and modeling, presenting and explaining new content for students. This phase is where you might use graphic organizers so that students can begin to interact with the content. For example, you might use a Venn diagram to compare the experiences of a Union and Confederate soldier or a KWL chart to examine dominant and recessive genes. Physical models (maps, models, and board games) or pictures are also important in this phase of instruction.

Graphic Organizers

Scan this QR code to download versions of these graphic organizers, and many more, to support active teaching.

Once the teach-and-model portion of the lesson is done, it's time for student collaboration. Student collaboration allows for students to come together to talk about new learning from the previous phase. In this phase, give students a structure to use for their interaction. Sentence stems or guiding questions can also be helpful. Tailor suggested sentence stems or questions based on the goal of the student collaboration. For instance, if students are comparing strategies to solve a math problem, a guiding question like "How do you decide which strategy to use for different problems?" could help focus the conversation. Sentence stems that provide a framework for offering an idea ("I can see how _____ would help if _____. What do you think?"), agreeing ("I agree with that idea because . . ."), and disagreeing ("I see your point, but for me . . .") prompt students to respond thoughtfully. If needed, use your reminding language to keep students on track.

The final phase of active teaching is facilitating reflection, an often overlooked but critically important piece of engaging academics. Remember how important it was for sixth graders to have the purpose and goal set out clearly at the beginning of the lesson? The same thing is true at the end. Reflecting on the learning process allows students to synthesize information to draw on later. Discussion activities, writing activities, and art activities are three modalities that can be used to build students' awareness of how they learn and to help them recognize the growth in their learning. Not simply a chance to recount information, this is an opportunity to think about the experience of learning.

Teacher-Guided and Independent Student Practice

After students have reflected on their learning, it's time for them to practice applying the new learning. There are two different types of student practice: teacher-guided and independent. One way to think of teacher-guided student practice is as a nongrading phase. You can use this opportunity to see if you need to reteach something or perhaps create a resource like an anchor chart to guide students. Though this is *student* practice, you still have an important role to play. You will be reminding students of the objective to help guide them, and the activity you choose for them to complete will provide structure and focus. Interactive learning structures are a way to solidify new learning and explore the content in a clearly defined way, so these structures can be useful during student practice.

Next, you will assess the students for readiness for moving to independent practice. Some of my favorite quick assessments are Fist to Five, exit tickets, observations from a lap around the room, one-word responses, and 3-2-1 (see box on next page). These formative assessments are meant to be quick measures for students to express their skill and confidence levels as you consider moving on to the next phase of practice.

Based on your assessments students may be ready to move on to independent practice, which is a great opportunity to offer choice to students. Choice can help students invest in what they are doing. Students might choose among:

- Answering a written question or recording an audio answer.

- Drawing a picture or model of new learning or writing a journal prompt from the perspective of someone else.
- Writing on paper or typing on a digital platform.

Once independent practice is complete, you can move on to closing the lesson.

> **Quick Formative Assessments**
> - **Fist to Five.** Give students a question that they will respond to by either showing fingers (with a fist being 0) or using a Likert scale on a survey to say how confident they are with new content. My go-to: "On a scale of 0 to 5, say how confident are you with what we just learned about, with 0 being 'I have absolutely no idea what we just learned,' 3 being 'I kind of get this,' and 5 being 'I've got this, and I'm confident about it.'"
> - **Exit tickets.** Use a quick question, a sentence frame, or a prompt to gauge understanding.
> - **One word.** Ask students to think of a one-word summary of what they've learned, and then have students share their answers. You can choose to allow repeats, or give students time to think of three options so they are prepared if someone uses their response.
> - **3-2-1.** This provides so many options! A common prompt I give students is "3 new things I learned, 2 connections I can make, and 1 question I still have."

Closing the Lesson

For lesson closure, you have many options. It can be helpful to have a set of activities to pull from. This strategy allows students to become familiar with the protocols and format of each activity as they are repeated, and it offers you a variety of choices to use to keep the activities fresh for your sixth graders. You might ask students to have a quick class discussion, partner students up for elevator speeches, complete an exit slip, play Beat the Clock, or a write a twenty-word summary.

No matter which method you choose, this is an opportunity to wrap up the lesson in an organized and purposeful way.

Lesson Closure Activities

- **Elevator speech.** Students have sixty seconds to summarize what they learned, as if they are an expert in the material.
- **Beat the Clock:** Ask a question, and then give students ten to fifteen seconds to confer with classmates before you randomly call on a student to answer.
- **Exit slip.** There are lots of options for exit slips. Here are a couple:
    1. Have students put their name and answer to a question on the slip, and turn it in on their way out the door.
    2. Have students put their name and any lingering questions they have on a card. Then they can drop the card in one of three bins, labeled "Got it," "More practice," and "I need support."

Connecting Students and Curriculum

As you find texts for your language arts students, craft word problems for your mathematicians, or guide students in historical discovery, work to allow students to see themselves in the material. Ask yourself:

- "What is the background of the authors students are reading, or the characters they read about?"
- "What are the names used in math word problems? Is it just Molly and Thomas, or is there a Guadalupe, Ahmed, or Li?"
- "Am I teaching history from just a majority perspective, or am I bringing in a variety of perspectives and histories?"
- "Is the science lesson student centered or teacher centered?"

Dig deeper into the material and allow students to feel connected to what they are learning. Connection breeds engagement.

Observing Students

Student observation is a strong tool in creating engaging academics and in creating a positive community. You can never make an assumption that a student knows content, a routine, or a procedure. Take time to walk the perimeter of your room, and be purposeful in interactions with students. Listen to group and partner discussions so you can make informed choices about your lesson, instruction, and teaching as appropriate for your students. If you teach the same lesson to different sections each day, you should find yourself making changes during each class to meet the needs of different groups of students. Lesson plans, whether written out more formally on a document, thought through in a planning book, or just jotted on a sticky note, are meant to be fluid and responsive to the needs of the students in front of you.

As you observe your students, you are not just listening to the words they speak. Body language can also be a big indicator for middle school students. Sixth graders are still learning how to express themselves and manage their emotions. Noticing that a student's shoulders droop or head tilts down can alert you that they are upset or concerned about something.

That's a cue to check in and see what's going on. If they are working on an assignment and start to get overly fidgety, or perhaps very forcefully erase or cross something out, they may be highly frustrated with their assignment and need redirection or a reminder. This can also be a great opportunity for a quick break; pause the lesson or work time and have students turn and talk to a partner for a moment. This gives students a safe way to check in with each other to see if their own thinking is on track.

One example of how observation can change your lessons is a recent experience that occurred in my social studies room. In talking about the origins of World War I, students were each given a paragraph to read and then were supposed to complete an interactive learning structure known as Jigsaws. As I watched my first class finish the article, I noticed a few groups struggling to complete the "jigsaw" portion of the activity. As I worked to encourage the groups, I noticed students starting to shift in their seats and almost fall in on themselves. I paused the activity, realizing that it had been a while since they had done group work, as we were recently back in person from distance learning. I asked the students to show me, by a hidden vote, how comfortable they were with the activity. Noting students were primarily uncomfortable, we shifted to partner work to make the activity less risky for them. In later sections, we started with the partner work, and classes had more success.

See the appendix, p. 198, for this and other interactive learning structures.

Observation is a powerful tool, but it is important to not jump to conclusions too quickly. As a reading teacher, I once observed a group talking during independent reading time. I made the assumption that talking meant they weren't focused on their books. When I went closer to use some redirecting language, I heard them discussing their books and recommending them to each other. In my time as a student, we were always supposed to stay seated and relatively quiet. It took a couple of years of teaching to realize that just because a student is fidgety doesn't mean they aren't paying attention. They may simply be trying to work out some tension or energy that is building up. When observing students, if you see a behavior that trips your internal bias, take a moment to think, "What need is this student trying to meet right now? Is their way of behaving doing any harm or contradicting our classroom expectations?" Sixth graders don't yet know how to advocate for themselves, so sometimes the choices they make are to fill a need they can't yet express. Observing them without judgment helps you support them and helps them learn what they need to be successful.

Final Word

In Chapter 3, we talked about high expectations leading to high outcomes. As you set your academic expectations for your students, remember that each student is different. What is a stretch or causes frustration for one student may encourage independent learning for another. Sixth graders have an intense sense of fairness, and when they notice differences, they are quick to shout, "That's not fair!" Eleven- and twelve-year-olds often need a lesson on the difference between "fair" and "equal." You might explain that in school "equal" has to do with everyone being treated the same way, while "fair" means all students get what they need. Consider having a prepared analogy to help support students in understanding this concept as you work to differentiate for your struggling readers, special education students, English language learners, and honors students. As you may vary your expectations for students, it is crucial that you don't let bias play a role. Rely on your observations of your students and collaboration with your colleagues to make sure you're setting appropriate expectations for your students—high yet attainable expectations that challenge them to grow and take academic risks.

> **Fair Versus Equal**
>
> An analogy can be helpful for students. A classic example is imagining that three students come to a teacher with different ailments: a scraped knee, a migraine, and a broken finger. The teacher responds in the same way to each student, offering each one an adhesive bandage. This response is equal because everyone is treated the same way, but is it fair? No, because only the student with the scraped knee has received the necessary care. How can we make it more fair? By offering each student the specific support they need so that all students can be safe, healthy, and successful.

Grade 7

When it comes to our subject area, we so often want to dive right in. It's understandable; this is what we know and what we do. It might feel familiar to us, but for our middle school students, it's all new: *new* social dynamics, *new* physical growth, *new* moral dilemmas, *new* ethical decisions, *new* academic demands—and doing all these things with a *new* burden of self-consciousness!

We best set our students up for success in the classroom when we take our time. This is especially true when delivering quality content to these twelve- and thirteen-year-olds. While we are often accountable to curriculum guides or maps, state and school standards, or learning benchmarks, remember that these are structures, not laws. As the classroom teacher, trust yourself to know what your students require to be successful and give yourself permission to pace the content based on their evolving needs. As our middle schoolers move through the new surroundings of young adolescence, we can support them by setting a reliable path to learning. In expecting students to be able to do things on their own, we miss the purpose of middle school. I've heard it from parents, coaches, and even colleagues: "They should just know how to do [fill-in-the-blank]." They have to learn these things somewhere, and often that place is the middle school classroom.

Lesson Design

In Chapter 3, we discussed setting up a positive community in our classrooms that promotes collaboration, cooperation, and support. Seventh graders want to be challenged, but they can also be terrified of failing or looking foolish in front of their classmates. When we take the time to establish a positive community, our seventh graders will be more likely to take risks and take on new challenges. To answer the question of how we can set high expectations for our twelve- and thirteen-year-olds, we should keep in mind the support they need to be successful. Remember also that "support" is not the same as the dreaded accusation of "hand-holding." We can and should hold all students to increasingly higher academic standards, but we have to remember the role we play in getting them there.

Here are some questions I ask myself before, during, and after a lesson:

- **Where is our starting point?** It's important to know what we're working with. This is where we can ask two additional vital questions: What do my students need to know? What do my students need to do to get there?

- **Which parts of the lesson are review, and how can I help remind students of the learning and then take it to the next level?** Ideally, we're building on prior knowledge or prior skills; even the introduction of new concepts is typically based on familiar patterns of learning.

- **Which parts are new, and how can I support students as they learn new information and new skills?** It's a good idea to remind ourselves that while it's not new to us, it is new to them. Think of it from their perspective: How might this piece of learning occur to them? What do they have to compare it to? Which concepts will need careful explanation, modeling, and practice, and which ones will be more intuitive for students?

- **How often and in what ways are my students accessing the learning?** Think about the different types of learners in your classroom, based on skill, need, preference, and experience.

- **How long will it take to get from our starting point to our endpoint?** This means that the appropriate amount of time can be allotted for the learning to take place prior to a summative assessment or culminating activity.

Active Teaching

Once we've answered these questions, we're ready to deliver the content using the three phases of active teaching. (See the overview to this chapter.) We begin by setting expectations and goals, giving clear directions, and pointing students toward a purpose for the learning. When students know how to operate in a given time and place, it can help alleviate the guesswork (and creative interpretation!) so that learning can happen. There have definitely been times when I've had a thoughtful and engaging lesson plan prepared that fell completely flat because I did not properly set my students up for success. Picture it like this: You bring your seventh graders to a table filled with delicious treats and give them no instructions. They push; they shove. Some take more than they could want or need. Others timidly hang back, wanting to get something but not knowing how. In the end, the table is overturned and goodie wrappers litter the floor. Some students have eaten more than their share; others have gotten nothing at all. The table was laid with good things meant for them, but the kids were not ready for it. Now imagine that same scenario, but one where you told them that the expectation was to approach the table single file, take one treat, and enjoy this special celebration as a group. How different would that experience be?

During the teach-and-model phase, we are preparing students to approach this table. Seventh graders walk that fine line between wanting to be independent and needing our support, especially when it comes to learning. We can help them with this balance by building these elements into our lesson plans. Learning experiences that respect a student's need to exercise their independence include things like individual work time, academic choice, and exploration.

> ### Motivating With Choice
> Offering academic choices to middle schoolers translates their developmental need for independence and choice into motivation to complete an academic task. Choices can be as simple as:
>
> - Work independently at your desk or at the counter.
> - Create a slideshow presentation or a poster board.
> - Study with flashcards or notes.

Student Practice and Exploration

Exploration is a wonderful way to engage students in learning. It's an opportunity for students to take risks and try something new on their own. One example that comes to mind is a story a colleague in the art department of my school shared. In one assignment, the seventh graders at our school created a diorama that depicted the memory of an elder. This colleague had a student who was interested in creating a stand for his box. (These dioramas were to be mounted on the wall, but the student wanted to be able to set it on a table.) My colleague gave this student a few pointers, some guidance, assorted materials, and let him go; it took a few tries, but in the end, the student accomplished his goal and fashioned a neat little cardboard stand for his box.

What I took from this story is that great things can come out of letting kids explore. If they are motivated (something that happens when they are also interested in the outcome), then they will persevere even through initial failure. Additionally, my colleague was open to new ideas; he probably knew exactly how to fashion a stand for this box, but he also knew that it would be a much more meaningful experience for this student to try on his own. And who knows? Maybe this student could teach his teacher something new too. In my own experience, this happens a lot with class discussions. I know what I want the kids to get out of each novel we're examining, but I often learn something new and insightful about the books I've read (and taught) dozens of times because the students in my class are seeing them with new eyes.

Giving seventh graders room to try and do on their own is developmentally appropriate, but we also have to provide plenty of structure and support in their learning. Specifically, twelve- and thirteen-year-olds do well with predictable patterns because predictability instills a sense of order in the flow of our curriculum. It also helps students to focus on their learning rather than try to guess what's coming next or be uncertain about why a part of a lesson is important ("Will this be on the test?"). In this way, students are not only having the opportunity to practice content on their own but also the social and emotional skills of accountability and responsibility that will allow them to engage in more independent work as they move into eighth grade and beyond.

One colleague in the language department in my school gives a quiz to her Latin students on the last rotation day in our schedule; her students know and expect that on this day they will be assessed on everything they learned from that rotation. As a result, they make a habit of preparing appropriately. Here are other ways in which we might build predictable patterns into in our teaching:

- Have a specific type of opening activity each day. (For example, Mondays are review, Tuesdays are practice sets, Wednesdays are word problems, and so on.)

- Begin a unit with an anticipatory set. (See the sixth grade section for more ideas.)

- End each unit with an assessment that has the same or similar structure.

- Use specific steps to resolve group conflict.

- Employ a feedback guide for peer editing and review.

Culturally Responsive Teaching

Over time in education, we have come to understand and respect that cultural diversity should be an integral part of the fabric of our schools. How do we make this authentic and not additional? Individual teachers and schools alike should first look to their student population for ideas to integrate cultural diversity into their programming. One year, early in my career, our school had a sizable international student population from China. We had no prior experience to draw on in working with these students, but our principal knew that the most critical starting point was in welcoming and getting to know our students. Naming was an important part of this; some students wanted to be called by their given names while others preferred to choose an English name. So we could get to know our

students better, a colleague organized a series of special lunches where our students brought in a dish from their hometown to share with the faculty. It was a unique opportunity to learn about cuisine from different regions of China and to get to know our students outside of the classroom setting. Each of us reworked our curriculum and lesson plans that year so that we could better accommodate our visiting students and give their classmates an opportunity to learn more about Chinese culture. For example, a science colleague enthusiastically dove into a unit on the numerous scientific contributions China has given to the world. Our art teacher swapped out a project for a unit on calligraphy. In English, we read short stories and poetry by Chinese and Chinese American authors. It was a special year for our school, and it demonstrated key points about cultural responsiveness:

- Cultural responsiveness requires us to let go of some things to make room for others.

- Cultural responsiveness means demonstrating a deep level of care and commitment to knowing and understanding our students.

- Cultural responsiveness is most authentic when it becomes part of the fabric of our schools, as opposed to being haphazardly incorporated as part of singular or isolated events.

Middle schoolers benefit greatly when we teach and model respect for cultures outside of our students' experience. Remember the fifth guiding principle this book is based on: "What we know and believe about our students—individually, culturally, developmentally—informs our expectations, reactions, and attitudes about those students." This is an age when students are deeply interested in what makes them (and others) different. Social divisions can run rampant among twelve- and thirteen-year-olds, but it can also be a time of celebration and embracing of differences. Using inclusive language in our classrooms is a way to model this for our students. For example, in our classroom, my students and I say things like:

- "We respect ideas and questions in this class."
- "We use kind and respectful language with each other."
- "Mistakes are how we learn."
- "You don't have to be friends, but you do have to be friendly."
- "Differences make us different, not divided."

And it is always "*our* classroom," not "*my* classroom."

Final Word

As teachers, our basic job is to deliver content and facilitate learning. As middle school teachers, we're also faced with the unique challenges of our students' social and emotional development as well as the myriad of physical changes they are experiencing. Additionally, there's the factor of time: when planning our teaching, most of us have asked ourselves, "How do I fit this in when I'm expected to cover all this curriculum by a certain date?" The investment we make in organizing our lessons, putting supportive structures in place, creating predictable learning patterns, and being culturally responsive in our schools directly leads to high engagement in learning. We find that not only are students prepared to enjoy the feast, but there is room at the table for everyone.

Grade

In his book *Drive*, Daniel Pink discusses the three factors that create intrinsic motivation: autonomy, mastery, and purpose. He makes a direct connection to students in today's collaborative environment. We can bring these three keys to motivation into our classrooms as we explore engaging academics:

- **Autonomy.** Trust students to address the assigned work with their peers.

- **Mastery.** Engage students with challenging, hands-on work to elevate important skills.

- **Purpose.** Provide meaningful content that helps students see connections to today's world.

I've applied these ideas in every grade I'd taught, but they become especially key to offering engaging academics in eighth grade.

Developmentally, we know that eighth graders are eager for independence, social connection, and challenge. They enjoy research, learning how things work, collaborating in small groups, and being in charge of their own decisions. They are creative, often able to accept and act on constructive criticism, and yet quick to turn their backs on work that doesn't feel relevant or connected to their lives. To engage eighth graders in academics, we can capitalize on these traits and offer robust, meaningful challenges that will capture their attention and motivate their interest.

Lesson Design

As educational contexts change and the communities around us evolve, project-based learning (PBL) has become an increasingly relevant part of K–12 instruction. The small-group learning in the PBL model is a powerful way the developmentally responsive teacher connects the needs of our middle school students with the goals we have as their learning facilitators.

> ## What Is Project-Based Learning?
>
> Project-based learning, or PBL, is far more than doing a project as a culminating event in a traditional unit of study. In PBL, the project doesn't simply demonstrate learning, it *is* the learning. A helpful comparison can be thinking about "dessert" projects versus "the main course" (PBLWorks n.d.).
>
> Dessert projects apply knowledge learned at the end of a unit, often by creating something like a poster or diorama as an illustration of students' learning. Main course projects connect to the real world, show students the meaning behind their learning, and motivate deep engagement. PBL consists of main course projects: long-term projects that drive students to develop knowledge and skills as they respond to their own questions and/or real-world problems.
>
> Some schools develop curriculum exclusively in a PBL model, but you can incorporate project-based learning into your curriculum no matter where or what you teach.

The more we integrate crucial social, emotional, and academic competencies, the better we can engage our students and involve them in their learning. When I sit down to plan a unit or project, one thing I keep foremost in mind is the eighth grader's need for agency (choice) and purpose (why it matters to them). Recently, I planned a monthlong project around two of my favorite learning models: design thinking and PBL (teachers get to have fun too!). The project was titled "Your Vote Matters—Designing a US President." Rather than being partisan, the concept was to identify the personal attributes and qualities of a commander in chief: powerful, intelligent, inspiring, empathetic, and so on. This project connected both social studies and English language arts, with a little math thrown in. Interdisciplinary projects like this are an ideal way to work with grade-level colleagues to design and develop an impactful and engaging integrated unit that takes important academic content and student interest into consideration.

The driving question of the unit was "What personal qualities contribute to your ideal US president?" If you think you hear purposeful envisioning language here, you are absolutely right! This brainstorming piece, when small-group members presented their ideas, validated the personal qualities important to them. Each individual student's presidential attributes were respectfully discussed and debated until a list of three personal characteristics and attributes were decided on by the group. This contribution was the hook the students needed to engage with the important work. With our support, our discerning students of today will develop into the discerning voters of tomorrow.

Active Teaching

Given the time I took to develop relationships early on in the year, as we progressed with our US presidents project, I divided the class into small groups that took social, emotional, and academic equity into consideration. The strong peer relationships that we developed helped create productive work teams and really addressed the heart of our active teaching in several important ways:

> **Benefits of Small Groups**
> - Support identity formation.
> - Meet students' need for belonging.
> - Increase individual effort and perseverance.
> - Reduce off-task behavior.

- **Students had efficient structure in group conversations.** It made it much easier to have a productive discussion, in which students discussed and compared what they had learned, and to take risks, support each other, and maintain peer status.

- **Students applied prompts and sentence stems in group work.** (See the sixth grade section, page XX, for some sentence stem ideas.) Small groups can more quickly begin equitable conversations than larger groups can.

- **Students developed effective listening skills.** On a daily basis, they practiced the essential life skills of focus, sustained attention, and comprehension.

- **Students provided targeted peer feedback.** As the students discussed, I circulated to guide, coach, and correct any misunderstandings. It's particularly effective if teachers talk less and listen more to honor students' independent thinking and agency.

Rather than the teacher being the sole source of high-quality, rigorous, and engaging instruction, it can be more relevant and valuable when the students deliver instruction to each other. Sometimes, students gain more clarity about a subject by repeatedly discussing it with their peers than they do from teacher explanations. What is more rewarding and engaging to an eighth grader than this type of agency? Watching it successfully unfold provides the moments that remind us why we teach.

Age-Appropriate Agency

The reality is that we as middle school educators are responsible for teaching our subject's content and ensuring we attain certain standards with our students. As developmentally responsive educators, we build in agency—the ability to choose one's direction—whenever possible so students can impact their own learning and establish a natural buy-in to the material. This concept of academic choice enters my projects within the small-group model in a few ways, starting by providing a structure in which students can ask questions and then eventually locate the resources with which to answer their questions and apply what they have learned.

We begin the process by establishing the subject and driving question (what we learn). This driving question often comes from the teacher. It's in the second phase (how we learn) that students can exercise more agency, including raising open-ended questions. I tell students that if they can find the answer through a simple online search, they should choose a different question! Offering academic choices supports the development of student agency in a few important ways:

- Carefully designed questions allow students to provide carefully considered answers and content.

- Teachers can guide by asking questions about the questions.

- Student questions tell us the direction of their thinking, allowing us to provide further guidance.

- Asking and responding to their peers' questions allows students to learn from others.

- Fostering this structure creates a habit of curiosity.

Using this approach, I have found that students' need-to-know questions reflect their authentic curiosity and determine the path of our future work. This open-ended structure, in which student interests guide the direction of the learning, answers the important middle school question, "What does this have to do with me?" and sets a productive tone to our work together.

Assessment

Learning is so much more than what we see on paper. Research supports a growing belief that using multiple measures of assessment is an effective way to truly gauge students' learning. Relatedly, one question that often comes up from others is "How do we grade work like this so we understand what students learned?" Rubrics are an effective tool for evaluation. The model is very flexible, and the best contain several key elements:

- Skill growth continuum
- Standards-based targets
- Social connection/collaboration
- Effort

It's easy to support our high expectations and reflect the levels of challenge within a well-designed rubric, and I adjust the rubrics I use to fit the needs and targets in each project. The beauty of a rubric is that it is endlessly easy to customize. In eighth grade, a carefully considered rubric evaluation can and should contain both student self-assessment and teacher observation. One caution: at this age, students are often harder on themselves that we are on them. A brief series of conferences with students helps us to calibrate feedback and support meaningful social-emotional and academic growth.

Not only does this flexible design support important student autonomy, but it also fosters self-awareness. It supports the ability of students to develop essential independent thinking, creating character qualities that benefit them and others.

Connecting Students and the Curriculum

Learning about our students is one step; continuing that connection is a journey. Every developmentally responsive teacher needs to first build a relationship with students before they can be effectively taught. (If you've read this far in the book, you've heard that a number of times!) A developmentally responsive relationship should evolve from talking *at* your students to teaching *with* them. In the introduction to this book, we mentioned one of our guiding principles: "What we know and believe about our students—individually, culturally, developmentally—informs our expectations, reactions, and attitudes about those students."

While it's easy to apply this principle to behavioral and social-emotional learning, consider the power when you do the same with our academic standards in eighth grade. Our students are ready to break free of us, to be unique individuals and yet connected to their peers. The time I take to get to know the whole child makes it easier to adjust the lessons toward subjects, applications, and assessments that are meaningful to them. While this may sound like yet more work, it provides the intangible gift to the student of being seen as a person rather than a name. It's exactly this environment that allows us, as their teachers, to provide the agency our eighth graders crave and helps them successfully transition into becoming successful young adults.

Culturally Responsive Teaching

One of the most powerful gifts we can provide our middle school students is a better understanding of the world. Many educators address cultural equity as an entirely separate subject rather than as an inherent, vital component of all we do. Purposeful culturally responsive teaching directly connects what students learn throughout all class content to the impact their learning has beyond the walls of the school. When we recognize, value, and teach about all cultures—in and out of our classroom—we elevate the history of these groups rather than erase it.

This idea supported another recent project that gave me an opportunity to blend some key developmental traits of this age—the desire for peer connection, creativity, and social justice—with my passion for cultural equity. The project was built around Sara Ahmed's book *Being the Change*. The relationships and community we built early in the year gave us the opportunity to dive into the hard work of social equity to tackle the skill I call "equity intelligence." Weaving in standards for reading, writing, social studies, we guided our eighth graders through reflective activities:

- "What makes me a unique individual?"
- "How does my past affect my present?"
- "Why do I believe things about others?"
- "What beliefs do I need to adjust?"
- "How can I use my cultural awareness to have a positive impact on others?"

In our student-centered classroom, we were able to tackle this equity work only after we had created an emotionally safe environment. The timeline that I sketched out for the project allowed us space and time to be honest and vulnerable with each other so we could explore the deep content. In sharing about themselves, the students made personal connections and discovered more about each other. We accessed resources specifically chosen to reflect cultural characters and situations that mirrored our students and their lives. This supported authentic class debates on the how and why of recent racial conflicts in our community and country; our eighth graders are ripe for this type of meaningful engagement. By doing the work to develop self-awareness, my students created and presented powerful equity outreach applications to the school and community that were important to them. Again, we incorporated choice into how students presented their work, with options to create artwork, posters, videos, writing, poetry, and learning demonstrations.

Final Word

In our diverse environment, it is simply a gift to show students this age a path toward an inclusive future built on understanding and compromise. By providing our students with ways to exercise their agency, they can model the power of inclusivity to others in impactful forms. As eighth grade educators, we need to remember that *our* culturally responsive teaching becomes *their* culturally responsive learning. Our collective openness, modeling, curiosity, and welcoming sets the tone for everyone around us. Rather than present them with thoughts and content, let's enrich them with new ways to think and act. That way, what they learn doesn't end when the bell rings—they will carry it with them during middle school and beyond.

Chapter 5
Connecting With Parents

Overview

Our classroom—including the community it embraces—is a special place, and ensuring that it provides a positive learning environment for our students is one of our most important tasks as educators. However, we also need to remember that our students are members of many other communities in addition to the one we establish in our classroom. Helping our students find real success goes far beyond managing a classroom well. It requires that teachers understand and partner with the most important community that a child belongs to: their family.

Extending the strong community of our classroom out to the homes our students return to each day demonstrates to our students that learning and growing doesn't stop when the bell rings. It also allows us to know and support our students better. Connecting with students' families, which might include parents, foster parents, grandparents, or guardians, involves much more than simply sending the occasional email or newsletter. The home-to-school connection is a bridge that allows us to partner with students' families to ensure students' success.

> **About the Term "Parent"**
>
> Students come from homes with a variety of family structures. Students might be raised by grandparents, siblings, aunts and uncles, foster families, and other caregivers. All of these individuals are to be honored for devoting their time, attention, and love to raising children, and we include all of them in our thinking in this chapter.
>
> It's difficult to find one word that encompasses all these caregivers and fits the importance of the role they play. In this book, for ease of reading, we use the term "parent" to represent all the caregivers involved in a child's life.

Parents as Partners

Families are our partners in their child's education. Parents and teachers need each other. We each contribute different strengths to the collaboration that is critical to educating middle schoolers. The most important thing to keep in mind is that the connection between home and school is not a one-way street. Families know their own children very well, and we can learn a lot from them. Families can share a great amount of knowledge about their children. They were, and are, their children's first teacher. They know what excites their children and what can stop them in their tracks. They know their children's passions, their worries, and the best way for them to learn. The insights and involvement of students' families are vital to understanding students' needs and experiences.

Similarly, teachers can provide insights that parents don't typically have about their own children. The middle school years are a time when students are developing more independence and are often eager to forge their own path. At the same time, as we've mentioned many times throughout this book, they are not yet ready to be fully self-reliant; they need support from the adults in their lives to grow and develop into independent young adults. At this point in their development, adolescents can also be moody and unpredictable as their personalities and behaviors change and mature. Parents often need guidance about how best to create structure for their middle schoolers, when to step back, and when to intervene. Parents know their children as individuals, but teachers are the experts in middle schoolers. Teachers know the right level of academic challenge, helpful goals and supports, and the developmental strengths and needs of their students.

Together, parents and teachers share the mutual goal of ensuring our students' success. Trust between a family and the school is essential for a student to succeed, and for parents and teachers to be able to work as a team, we need to establish a sense of trust as soon as possible. You will set yourself up for success if you can ensure that your communication with families engages them with a strong sense of empathy and with a clear intention of building this partnership. So how can we approach this communication in ways that are authentic and meaningful?

Communicating Trust

When we discussed teacher language in Chapter 3, we focused on what we say to students and how we say it. The same ideas apply to all of our communication about our students. When we connect with families, we need to ensure that what we say and how we say it demonstrates our level of care for and understanding of our students and their families. Here are some guidelines to keep in mind:

- **Engage as equals.** What we communicate to families often includes unfamiliar educational language and concepts. We must be sure to define the educational terms we utilize when discussing their child's status. It may help to provide visuals that are family friendly to explain concepts, such as graphs to show growth or progress. Just as we differentiate with our students, we can do the same with families. We can also help families understand the developmental context in which we work with their children. In Chapter 1 we spoke of child and adolescent development, and families will benefit from understanding where their child is currently and what they might expect to see in the near future.

- **Know your students' families.** We must seek to learn more about our families as we continue to teach their children. Being sure we know their names as well as who they are as people can help us with our daily interactions with their children, and this knowledge builds trust between you and your families. The best way for teachers to achieve this goal is to truly listen when talking with families. Remember that these conversations are a two-way street; you have goals for their children, and so do families. What are they trying to tell you?

- **Recognize family contributions.** So much of what we do with our students depends on the support of our students' families. For instance, when we work with students to set goals, we can partner with their families to help growth occur. We focus on the goal at school while the families focus on it at home. When we actively partner and recognize the work that families contribute, it fuels continued family engagement. Students make more progress this way too!

Connecting With All Families

How do we establish good communication with all of our students' families? While some families are eager to connect with their child's teacher and are ready to attend any event at any time, some families can be difficult to reach. To establish strong connections with families, we need to consider how we communicate in general. Many schools have expectations and requirements for teachers in terms of communication, including the format and frequency of messages. Often, we will need to go above and beyond our school's expectations in order to foster strong relationships with all our families. What works well for some families may not work for all families. Just as we do with our students, we need to meet families where they are. How and when we reach out to families can have a great impact on the responses we receive. Take into account what is comfortable for you and what works for your students' families, and be clear about how you will communicate. Consider the following:

- **Format.** There are so many possibilities for communication: in-person meetings, phone calls, Zoom meetings, emails, texts, blogs, newsletters, and more. Each one has its place and its purpose, and it's up to you (with consideration of any requirements your school has) to choose the formats that work best for you. Keep in mind that the quickest and most convenient methods of communication are not always the best formats for sensitive topics.

- **Time.** You will likely receive messages from families at all hours of the day, but for your own well-being, you shouldn't respond to messages at all hours. Let families know when the best time to reach you is (before and after the school day, perhaps) and when you won't be able to respond (during the school day while you're teaching, for instance, or after a set time in the evening). Being clear about these guidelines will help establish respectful communication.

- **Frequency.** Be consistent about your communication so families know how often they will hear from you. For example, you can establish that you will send an update via email every two weeks, or that you will have a new blog post every month. Consistency builds trust and sense of safety.

- **Length.** Keep communications brief and to the point, positive and focused. A good rule of thumb is that if an email to an individual family is longer than a couple of paragraphs, it's probably easier to pick up the phone and call.

- **Feedback.** Ask families to join the conversation. Offer opportunities for feedback through surveys or questions in your regular communications, and make sure that families know they can always reach out to you with questions or concerns.

- **Empathy.** Providing an understanding ear for your families will help build a trusting relationship. A family will be much more likely to join you as a partner if they feel that you care about them, and their child, on a personal level.

Building Positive Family Communities

These positive family relationships impact our classrooms in profound ways. The connection begins with the educator; your initial communication sets up the idea that this relationship lasts all year, and maybe beyond. Open, honest lines of communication are the first step in ensuring a healthy, helpful connection with your students' families. That isn't to say that it's always easy to do, however. Parent communication can be challenging at times, but it's always important.

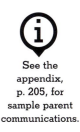

See the appendix, p. 205, for sample parent communications.

Your connection with families might include communication that builds and maintains relationships and a sense of community and that conveys information about classroom or school events. This information is important but general; it pertains to all families in a given class or grade level. Families are empowered, however, when they understand what is being taught in their child's class, and why. A family with knowledge of what is being taught each day can take part in maintaining the excitement, motivation, and energy necessary for a student to overcome difficult tasks and challenges.

You might include such information in a routine email or newsletter. These formats also provide a useful way to offer suggestions that will help parents connect with and support their children at home. For instance, families can help a student maintain their momentum by utilizing a schedule. Many times families may not know how to establish this practice, and we can share our experience and knowledge to help them.

There is also a need for more personalized communication with individual families. While this level of connection is more time-consuming on the teacher end, it's deeply impactful in terms of connecting with families and supporting students. Teachers often need to report or follow up on an issue related to progress or behavior. This communication often happens when something isn't going well—a student has gotten a poor grade on an assignment or has misbehaved in class. These moments are some of the most important partnership opportunities with families as we seek to understand what is going on for the student and how we can provide better support.

Additionally, it's important to remember to communicate when good things happen. Sending a message offering positive feedback about a student's progress or behavior, even if it's just a quick few sentences, can go a long way in helping a parent recognize that you see and appreciate their child.

● ● ● ● ● ● ● ● ●

Throughout this chapter, you will learn more about how our connections with families enriches students' experiences. Each grade-level section discusses a slightly different aspect of this home-school partnership. The sixth grade section offers guidance for in-person parent-teacher meetings, while the seventh grade section offers tips on virtual conferences. The eighth grade section provides ideas for learning more about students' families and using that knowledge to personalize home-school partnerships. No matter what grade you teach, you will find relevant practices and approaches described in each section.

Before we venture into each of the middle school grade levels, it's worth repeating that our familiarity with student's families strengthens that sense of community we work so hard to create within our classrooms. Regular communication helps us to understand where our students come from, both individually and culturally, and this knowledge is essential in creating an equitable classroom community. We will work with a diverse group of students and families throughout our teaching career, and we can always seek to learn more about the students we serve. A good communication practice between teachers and families helps create a positive environment for each student to enjoy.

Grade

The classroom is set up, your lessons are planned (at least for the first few days), and you are feeling ready to meet your sixth graders in person. It would seem everything is covered, but there is one more component to address. Teaching is much more than what goes on in your classroom. Partnering with families—knowing them and valuing their contributions— is as important as knowing the children we teach. Many teachers see the value in this idea, but putting it into practice can be intimidating.

Before School Begins

Before the year starts, families, just like their sixth graders, may be approaching the new school year with nervous excitement. While some districts and schools may send a lot of communication at the start of the school year, others send hardly any at all. It is helpful to connect with your principal to find out what sort of communication is happening in the lead-up to the first day of school. You can then keep that in mind as you plan your own next layer of outreach.

One requirement at my school is that teachers call the families of all the students in their advisory class before the first day of school. The idea is to make a connection, answer questions, and introduce ourselves before we start school. It takes effort, but making these phone calls over the course of a couple of days gives me a welcome opportunity to connect with my future advisees' families. I am able to address any concerns that are on their minds, and I am able to ask parents and guardians a few questions of my own. There may be too many students in your content area for you to call all families—some middle school teachers may teach hundreds of students a year—but focusing on students in your advisory or homeroom is a manageable place to start.

Many teachers also put together a welcome letter or email to send to students' families. In addition to introducing themselves as the teacher and sharing some information about the class, this communication provides a personal touch before the school year begins. You can also add another layer by asking for something in return to start building that relationship with families. Perhaps you'd like to know what they feel is one of their child's gifts as well as one of their challenges or what their wish is for their child for the coming school year. Families are the experts on their children, so use that to your advantage!

Making Time for Regular Communication

When connecting with families, it is also important to remember that their schedules and availability may be different from what we expect. Early in the school year, connect with families and ask them how they prefer to be contacted. (In the eighth grade section, you'll find additional ideas for family survey questions.) Making the effort to find out what works best for the adults in your students' lives is a small way to show that you care and are aware that "one size fits all" doesn't work effectively for students or their families.

There are some families that want a quick blast of information, while others prefer all the details you can provide. Although there will always be times that you will have to call a parent who prefers email, or vice versa, you should still make an effort to honor their request as much as you can. As you begin emailing, calling, and interacting with families, make note of these different styles. Print a roster of students that includes their parents' names, preferred mode of communication, and additional notes about the student or family.

Special Concerns of Sixth Grade Parents

Teaching can be a time-consuming profession, but putting in the effort to communicate about common questions up front helps set everyone up for success. Sixth grade families and students are learning a new way to "do" school. Students have more teachers than they did in elementary school, they must manage passing time between classes and the use of lockers, they have more independence in the classroom, they are dealing with increased levels of homework, they are aware that their families have access to the teacher's online gradebook, and they have many more opportunities to participate in after-school clubs, activities, and sports—and these are just a few of the new experiences in middle school. It is worth communicating with families and students early and often regarding a few key questions:

- **What is your policy for responding to adult communication?** For instance, I say I will respond within twenty-four hours, during the school day. I do mention that email is the fastest form of communication, but that I am also available by phone.

- **When do you update your gradebook?** This may be every day, it may be once a week, and it may change weekly. I have chosen Tuesdays to do a mass grading session (even if I have to take a few things home) to make sure the gradebook is as up-to-date as it can be on that day.

- **How often do you check for, and grade, late work?** This can be an especially stressful topic for students and their adults. The adult checks grades and notices something is missing, but the student promises they turned it in and it just hasn't been graded yet. Perhaps you have time each day to do this, or, like me, you set a "within one week of being turned in" policy to give yourself some space for things that come up. Be prepared for frequent emails from families about late and missing work in sixth grade, and know that it comes from a place of care and concern regarding their student's success.

> **Keeping Families Informed About Grades**
>
> Many schools use an online gradebook where families can access and see their student's grades. If they do not, consider how you will help families access this information. Perhaps your grade coordinates a grade-check email sent to your advisory families once a week, or a copy of grades, along with a list of missing work, is sent home on paper.

Share your approach to these essential questions with families right at the start of the school year. It can also be helpful to have a conversation about them with your grade-level teammates. You may find that you all have similar expectations, which can help all stakeholders navigate the transition to sixth grade more smoothly.

The Benefits of Positive Communication

From my experience, there is a lot more regularly scheduled communication in elementary school than in middle school. Middle school is a time for increased independence, for families as well as students. Some parents are used to a weekly letter or a folder that goes back and forth. These routines are often removed in sixth grade, and on top of that, students have many more teachers than they did in elementary school, which can make it more challenging for families to navigate the communication process. Think about when and why you might communicate with families. Will you send out missing assignment reminders once a week, every few weeks, or none at all? I scaffold this and do more at the start of the year and less as the year goes on, and I tell families to expect that.

Especially at the beginning of the school year, it's important for positive communication and connection to be established between home and school. When the only calls or emails a parent receives are negative (for example, about attendance, grades, missing work, or behavior concerns), it chips away at the relationship between home and school. When will you find moments to communicate with families for positive reasons? Perhaps once a grading period, reach out with an observation about how it's going for their child. These positive connections can also be a way to help you connect with families when it's time for them to come to school for conferences or parent-teacher meetings.

Parent-Teacher Conferences

When I first started teaching, I was so intimidated by parent-teacher conferences. I still get a little nervous about them, but it helps to remind myself that everyone sitting at that table is there to support the student; they all want the student to do their best and be successful. The family is the expert on the child, and you are the expert on your content and in your role as educator. The purpose of the conference is to come together to discuss how the student is doing, including their areas of strength and areas for growth.

Over the years, I have participated in a variety of conference formats: scheduled for all students, invite only, open houses, and unscheduled. There are a few strategies that make any parent-teacher meeting more successful:

- **Open with gratitude.** These families are taking time out of their schedules to come meet with you. As a sixth grade parent, and especially if the child is their eldest, this is new territory. Greet them with a smile, a firm handshake (if culturally appropriate), and introduce yourself. Thank them for joining you and invite them to sit.

- **Start with a purpose (and a time limit).** Your school administrators may give a general purpose, and you should share that goal, or your own, with families as you sit down together. For instance, you might say, "Today we have twenty minutes scheduled to talk about how school is going for Sam during the transition to sixth grade and answer any questions that have come up for you."

- **Remember it's a conversation.** You are not talking to the family, you are talking with them. They know their child and have a wealth of knowledge about them outside of the walls of your classroom and school. It should be a back-and-forth dialogue, not a monologue.

- **Create an action step.** Ending the conference by identifying an action step makes the time more purposeful and can help guide the next conversation. I have found that asking families, "What can I do to better support ___?" helps me create my action step. There is also always something the student can do to grow, and you can frame that as "My action step is to ___. Before our next check-in, your action step as a family is to ___."

- **Leave on a positive note.** There will be difficult conferences with families. A student might really be struggling academically, there might be family matters affecting the learning, or perhaps there is a difficult behavior you needed to discuss. No matter what, remind yourself that you are all there for the same purpose, and working together will help the student to make progress. You started your conference with a warm welcome, so be sure to end it with a positive: "Thank you for joining me and talking about ____'s progress" or "I appreciated your time this evening to talk about how we can best support ____ at school."

- **Follow up.** If you have a moment to send a quick email to the family a day or two after your conference, it goes a long way in cementing your positive partnership. It can be three sentences: reiterate your thanks for their time, make a positive connection about their child, and close with encouragement to reach out to you with any questions. When families feel that they, and their child, are seen and appreciated, they are much more willing to partner with you.

Difficult Conversations

There are always tricky conferences or conversations in middle school! Often, this type of conversation comes up not at a scheduled conference but rather in a phone call or unplanned conference with families. During these conversations, it is crucial that you as the teacher stay calm, open, honest, and empathetic. Do your best to keep your ego out of it, because the conversation should be about the student, not you. The parent's job is to advocate for their child and they are doing so with the information they have available (often what their child is telling them). Throughout the conversation, try to maintain a calm voice, even if you have to take a deep breath here and there. Throughout the conversation, share the facts and try not to share your opinion. Make notes in a communication log in a notebook or digital document so you can refer back to it during your next scheduled conference. ("I know we talked on March 3 about Taylor's missing math class. Since then, they've been to math every day that they've been in school.") Let parents finish their thoughts during the conversation; listen to what they have to say without interjecting or interrupting, and answer their questions to the best of your ability. You want them to feel heard and to leave without any lingering confusion.

Depending on how complicated a conversation you are having, it's possible that solutions may take more than one meeting to achieve. In that case, end the conversation in the same way we discussed earlier: with action steps and follow-up. You might finish up by saying, "My next step is to meet with Taylor after school to go over the lesson from the missed class. At the end of this week, I'll let you know what they should work on to prepare for next week's quiz. Let's plan to check in again after the quiz to see how everything is going." Make sure to follow up later as promised, and keep an up-to-date record so you will be prepared for future conversations.

Final Word

Your early efforts to reach out to families and the rapport you establish will help set a foundation for positive collaboration. As an educator, you hope every phone call and email with families will go well. However, sometimes communication wires get crossed, and there will be times you need to loop in an administrator. It may mean just notifying your administrator about how the conversation went and asking them for some feedback and ideas so you can reach back out to the family. Sometimes, the administrator may want to contact families or hold a team meeting. No matter which one of these scenarios unfolds, it is important that you keep your administrator informed so that they are well positioned to help the student, their family, and you.

Parents and guardians, the adults entrusted with the care of our students, are some of the greatest allies a teacher has. They know the student and advocate for them, and they are also there to work with you to create the best educational experience for their child. You are a part of this student's team, and it is a gift to be included. Be sure that you also include the parents in your classroom through open and authentic communication.

Grade 7

Any good relationship starts with communication, and good communication starts with listening. We want to have positive, working relationships with our students' families so that we can partner in helping students navigate through middle school. Simple advice, but where to start? Few of us are taught how to reach out to the families of the students in our care. We put so much careful thought and consideration into investing in our students; how do we best invest in their parents and guardians?

Before School Begins

Ideally, a starting point is to reach out to families before their students even walk through our classroom doors. They would learn some things about us, what to look forward to in our respective classes, and what our expectations are for their children. We would offer them multiple means of communication and extend an invitation to share with us key pieces of information that will help us to best serve their child. We would have opportunities to listen to their concerns and answer their questions before the first day of school. While this would be the ideal, we know that in reality it is not always feasible to connect with the family of every single student on our rosters, much less lay the foundation for a working relationship with them. Still, the more we can connect with families at the beginning of the school year, the better for us and all the better for them. A simple welcome email or postcard home can open up our classroom not only to our students, but to their families as well.

Making Time for Regular Communication

Parent communication can be a challenging process to get right, but investing the effort in it is time well spent. It truly does help us to better connect with and teach the children in our care. While there are some families you may not connect with often, others will benefit from and greatly appreciate regular communication. There will be students in your class who have challenges or problems that require the partnering of school and home. As we have to do with so many of our responsibilities in the classroom, it is wise to set ourselves up for success. Here are some tips to consider:

- **Make the first point of contact a positive one, and as specific to the child as possible.** Reaching out to families in a warm, welcoming way sets a positive tone for the start of the school year. Additionally, sharing a positive comment about their child shows that you care about the child's well-being. This is especially helpful when future communication with them is about academic concerns or behavioral issues; when a problem is the first point of contact with a parent, it can be difficult for them to see you as an ally.

- **Check in regularly.** When I reach out to families, I'm always surprised by how many parents reply with a question or concern that they might not have otherwise brought to my attention. All it takes is an opportunity to connect, and a conversation is started! A routine check-in might be as simple as a quick email home each quarter sharing highlights from class, a peek at what's ahead, and an invitation to reply with any questions, comments, or concerns.

- **Ensure that families feel seen and welcome in your classroom.** Think about how you make your students feel welcome through belonging, significance, and fun. Parents and guardians are no different. Your classroom should be a safe place for them to bring their concerns or listen to yours, even if the conversation is happening online or on the phone rather than in person.

- **As much as we can, we should know our parents by name.** This is easier when you have a small group of students assigned to you (as in an advisory group or homeroom). At the very least, be sure to know their name when contacting them or when they reach out to you so that you can properly address them. Remember that not all children share the same last name as their parents or guardians; it's a sign of respect that you take the time to look up their preferred name or to ask.

Special Concerns of Seventh Grade Parents

If a child is going to have a difficult year in their middle school experience, it will most likely be in seventh grade. A quick article search online for "seventh grade" results in page after page with titles along the lines of "A Parent's Guide to Surviving Seventh Grade," "Why Seventh Grade Is So Difficult," and "Why Seventh Grade Is the Worst." There are difficulties and challenges in any transition, and that is what seventh grade is: a critical year for children and one of tremendous (and sometimes tumultuous) change and growth.

In sixth grade, middle school is still new, students are eager to do well and please the adults in their lives, and students generally tolerate one another. By seventh grade, most students have developed beyond childhood and well into their young adolescence. Remember the developmental characteristics discussed in Chapter 1: seventh graders are primarily motivated by social factors, are deeply influenced by their peers, and can fall into conflicting relationships with adults (in one moment wanting their help, while in the next moment horrified by their very presence). This is a normal, if challenging, phase of their development—and if we're seeing it at school, their family is very likely experiencing it at home too!

Additionally, the academic experience shifts in seventh grade. Students who once loved school and excelled in most subjects without really trying are suddenly faced with increasingly specific content areas (especially in areas like math and languages) that require them to utilize study skills and academic competencies they previously had not had to think about much. For many students, grades might start to slip around October or November.

To top it all off, there are physical changes that can rock our seventh graders' worlds: some experience delayed growth while others have literal growing pains; many endure the devastating introduction of braces; and others begin to experience emotional issues including depression, anxiety, and stress. Phew! It's no wonder that one of the top internet searches for "Why is seventh grade . . ." is autocompleted with ". . . the hardest year?"

As educators and parents in the lives of these students, we can be stretched and tested (and at times frustrated!), but having come out on the other side of seventh grade ourselves, we are well equipped to guide our students through the joys and challenges of this year. When interacting with parents, it's important to remember that their personal experiences in school may have been stressful or challenging too. As they experience seventh grade again through their children, they sometimes relive those difficult moments. It is all the more important, then, that we listen carefully to parents and partner with families to ensure that our students are receiving the best care.

Taking Proactive Steps

Being proactive in these situations will mean a swift resolution or at least a road toward "better" for the child. While we know that "this too shall pass," it is not helpful to say such things to our students when they are in the thick of it. Instead, families and teachers can partner as navigators pointing them toward growth. Reaching out to parents early on will also ensure that the issue does not get worse; we want to avoid the snowball effect when it comes to academic or behavioral concerns.

One key is to separate the child from the concern. In your conversations with families about problems or concerns, try to share as many specifics as you can to promote an active, engaged school-home partnership. You might first share what the concerns are and when they occur ("I've noticed that Alex has been behaving differently when working in small groups. He's been acting frustrated toward his classmates"), as well as the effect this is having on the child and others ("When he behaves in this way, he separates himself from his classmates and his work ends up being incomplete"). Mentioning the steps you've already taken to support the child is a helpful way to demonstrate to parents that you are a true partner for them. Then, asking for their input ("Have you noticed anything similar at home? Is there anything else I can do to support Alex in the classroom?") and suggesting solution-based next steps lay the groundwork for effective collaboration.

This communication demonstrates empathy, but does not let go of accountability. The teacher is still holding Alex to a high standard, but also reaching out to Alex and his parents with viable solutions that could prevent a more difficult situation.

The Benefits of Positive Communication

While we could easily get bogged down with the challenges of seventh grade, remember that there are so many joys and triumphs. Parents want to be part of that, too. As outlined in the overview to this chapter, we also want to communicate with parents the positive happenings, not just the problems or concerns. It's so easy to focus on what isn't going well, but it's equally important to capture what's working. Our minds might go to our high achievers, and while we want to acknowledge and recognize their strengths and hard work, it's also valuable to reach out to families when a child who has been struggling shows genuine progress. When a child who has consistently been making Ds on assessments works hard for a C, that's a victory that all stakeholders in a child's life want to share. It encourages students, parents, and teachers, too. It's a wonderful experience to be able to write a positive note about a child instead of a difficult one.

Difficult Conversations

When we do have concerns we need to bring to a family's attention, it's advisable to tread cautiously—we shouldn't presume what they know about their student's experience at school. A family might be observing the exact same behaviors that you are bringing to their attention, or what you have to share with them might be completely overwhelming or surprising. In either case, frame the conversation as best you can, taking into account what you know about the parent's view of their child, so that you can communicate the concern and begin working on a solution. Remember that while it may not be personal for you, it is deeply personal for families. This is their child, after all. Additionally, many parents and guardians see their children as a reflection of themselves. We can help guide them through this age by reminding them of the developmental characteristics of young adolescents. (See Chapter 1.) Mistakes are expected, and framing them as such can help steer a child (and their parents) toward a solution.

While we can create action plans at school, it's important to remember to respect what works for families at home, even if it does not align with your personal beliefs. Home and school are connected by the parent-teacher relationship, but distinctly separate. With that in mind, we should approach difficult conversations by restating goals, remembering not to take things personally, having empathy for families, and recognizing parents' rights to raise their children the way they think is right (within the bounds of the law, of course).

The choices we make in the classroom in terms of management, discipline, and building positive community may be in conflict with what families believe is right, correct, or appropriate for the rearing of their child. Students or parents might even bring up these differences, saying things like "That's not how we do things at home" or "At home, we can say [or do] those things." I make a very clear distinction with my students: "In this class, we do _____." "In this class, we say _____." "In this class, we will be _____ to one another." Unless it is harmful or dangerous for the child, we need to work in partnership with their parents, and that means respecting their wishes for how their child is to be raised.

> **Mandatory Reporting**
> We always need to be alert to instances of abuse or neglect and immediately report suspicions or evidence to the appropriate authorities both at your school and in your state.

For example, I taught a student whose family has their children go on runs when they misbehave at school or receive poor grades. I've also had families that were totally permissive of a child's behavior at home. There are families that are in denial about their child or blame others (including the school) for their child's struggles. When it comes to cases like these, I make sure I've communicated what I can to the family and then come up with a plan for how to deal with the issues at school.

We can only control what happens in our sphere of influence, and for many of us, that is limited to the classroom. Raising children is highly influenced by culture, and inevitably, you will partner with parents whose approaches don't align with your own ideas about child rearing. A veteran teacher told me early in my career: "Everyone gets to raise their child the way they think is right." Sometimes teaching feels like parenting, which is why we can feel so strongly about certain aspects of a student's upbringing. While some of us may be like surrogate parents to some students, it is really important that we remember our role in our students' lives; for most of them, we are teacher, coach, disciplinarian, advisor, chaperone, mentor. You can't tell a parent how to parent, but you can share with them things that work in the classroom that they might find helpful.

A good question to ask when faced with a tricky situation is "Who is the right person to help this child?" Sometimes that will be you, the classroom teacher. This is especially relevant if the concern is about an academic matter or a behavioral issue in class. Some concerns will require you to reach out to the school counselor, psychologist, nurse, dean of students, or administration. Know your school's or district's resources and protocols before the school year starts. As issues arise, ask your administrator if you are unsure of how to proceed. This will ensure that the child is getting the appropriate care.

Connecting Virtually With Parents

In the sixth grade section, we talked about how to hold productive and positive parent-teacher conferences. Here, we'll focus on how to connect with parents when the meeting is virtual. The goals are the same: communicate with honesty, care, and compassion, maintain professionalism, be solution oriented, have an action plan, and demonstrate that you know the child as an individual.

- **Prepare parents and students.** Make sure they know which video-conferencing platform to use, how to find you (a step-by-step guide or video is helpful!), and when to meet you. Overcommunicate these details well in advance, and again the day before the conference.

- **Set up your tech.** Check internet connectivity, charge your devices, and log on to the virtual platform before the meeting is set to start.

- **Be prepared.** Have everything you need within reach: conference preparation forms, student work, notes, reminders, and an outline of the items to cover. Set up your command station. Having water within reach is a must for me; your area might include coffee, a favorite pen, a fan, and so on.

- **Think about the virtual view.** Just as we set up our classrooms to be safe and inviting spaces, we should set up our virtual space in a way that makes parents feel comfortable and welcome. Consider your camera choice, camera angle, lighting, clothing, and the visible background.

- **Have a back-up plan.** It's Murphy's law: "Anything that can go wrong will go wrong." Maybe the internet connection is spotty. Perhaps you didn't know you would need a translator. Be prepared with alternative ways you can reach out to these parents.

Final Word

Partnering with parents has countless benefits; there is a strong body of evidence that supports the correlation between parent-teacher communication and a child's academic performance. Teachers and parents who communicate ensure that students' academic, social, and emotional needs are being monitored and met. This partnership also communicates to students that there are many adults in their lives who care about them. I use the phrase "It takes a village" so often with colleagues and parents because truly, it does! No one can do this job alone. I'm always deeply grateful when I can count parents as part of my village—and no matter how often seventh graders roll their eyes about it, they appreciate it too.

Grade

Positive and productive family communication is established on a foundation of common understanding. When families come to me with questions, I apply the approach of listen more, talk less. I take notes to show their questions and concerns matter (and to provide me with good records!). Many times, they ask questions because they need to know how to better understand the material or measure progress. Or they may have had negative experiences with classroom teachers, school leaders, or district administration in the past, prompting their need to establish a presence ("I'm here. Don't forget me!"). Your responsive attention sets an expectation of open communication from the start.

Beginning-of-the-Year Survey

From day one, I work to learn about families. As mentioned in the seventh grade section, it takes a village to do this work, and the more we learn about each other, the stronger that village community grows. I strive to look for bright spots—positive opportunities, events, or moments. The more true interest I take in students' families, the brighter our relationship becomes, and the better parents learn to see themselves as our partners as we walk alongside each other to support the success of their child.

At the beginning of every year, I send home a simple, four-question survey to families (these days, it's most often via online forms, but paper works too) to fill out at home, during a back to school night, or whenever I can grab a few minutes of their time. On this survey, I ask things like:

- "What priority do you have for your child this year?"
- "What has been your best experience during your child's education?"
- "What do you wish I knew about your child?"
- "How do you prefer to be reached? (Email? Text? Phone?)"

Questions like these help us understand parents' emotional center. Even if you don't hear from them, families appreciate the effort. And if you do hear from them, you have a place to start building a relationship.

Make the Most of Small Moments

Connections with families should be sincere, display authentic personal interest, and be kept brief. Let's face it: everyone is juggling multiple responsibilities these days. Simple questions such as "How are you today?" or "How is your mother doing?" go a long way to let parents know they are a meaningful part of the school community.

The special sauce for these relationships is intentionally taking the time to learn the names of a student's siblings, extended family members, favorite activities, and even pets. (I take notes on all of these details and use them whenever I can.) These tidbits of information show that you have taken the time to listen and remember because you genuinely care. You'll see an eighth grader's eyes light up when you ask about their dog by name, and you'll have a quick conversation starter for parents when you can inquire about your student's younger sibling or their recent trip to see a grandparent. These seemingly small moments of social and emotional communication provide a bit of warmth that may be rare in their lives or in their past experiences of parent-teacher communication. When there are more difficult moments, these family members will remember when you were there with your support. Be a bright spot for them.

Be a Window Rather Than a Mirror

We often think about how our students are transitioning to their new position in school and increasing workload, but remember that their families are transitioning as well. Just as we work to create independence in our eighth graders, we can do the same for parents through transparent family communication. There are several areas to consider:

- **Structure.** Their child's data, schedule, assignments, progress, and so on should be as accessible as possible. When the experience of providing this information is new to families, I respectfully offer step-by-step directions, delivered in person, by video, or in writing, about how to access information via the school learning management system. For families with limited technology or language access, I've used grants to create a place at school for access to a laptop so they can learn a new skill and check on their child's data. This is a great opportunity to empower them to learn a new and crucial practical skill and help them feel more connected to the school, and it's also an enriching way to involve students, who can exercise leadership skills by acting as tech coaches for these families. In our case, it became our school's own "internet café," which made everyone feel more at home.

- **Curriculum.** "This is so different from my day." It's a common refrain. Families can be confused by, or even resistant to, the curriculum, classroom management, or teaching models we use. Regardless of where or when the adult voicing this concern grew up, it's an issue that deserves our empathetic response. I do three things: First, I review the developmental basics and provide reasons why we do what we do. Second, I connect their goals for their child (remember that survey?) to the work in our class. Third, we discuss exactly how the curriculum content directly connects to the increasing rigor and workload of high school. Charts, tables, and other visuals are helpful here, and have copies ready for families so they can take them home.

I bring these approaches together as I show families, for example, how the productive struggle of completing a few relevant academic assignments helps students develop the perseverance and logic that they will need to achieve their goal of, say, learning software engineering or auto repair. Relatedly, finding a real-life use for the vibranium in the movie *Black Panther* connects to the student's aspirations to explore chemistry in high school and college. The concepts in our curriculum can often be presented as ways that respond to both the students' academic needs and the social and emotional requirements of an ever-changing world. Learning shifts often occur when we take time to reframe an idea.

- **Development.** Eighth graders can present a conundrum. Our students push away parents and seek deeper connections to peers. They continue to crave an independent identity and look for adult approval. During these middle school years, the lightning speed with which children change in size, intellect, maturity, and social awareness surprises families. Regular emails, discussion, and parent education about the subject of eighth grade development, along with take-home resources, can be invaluable. A little front-loading goes a long way in creating comfort for everyone.

- **Family issues.** Families often come to us with worries that can turn into big problems. Be prepared for questions like:

    - "How can I both stay involved and give my child more autonomy and independence?"

    - "How often should I step in or leave something alone (for example, missing assignments, time management, self-advocacy)?"

    - "How can I support my child in learning how to proactively take care of school problems before they get too big (failing, dropping grades, too many missing projects and assignments)?"

Of course, there are no right, one-size-fits-all answers to these questions. Our empathetic responses to questions like these change student by student, year by year, always guided by what we know about those families and students. The more open and honest we are with our answers, the more strongly families trust our knowledge and support.

Addressing Concerns

Creating an environment of mutual problem-solving (because there will be problems) is the first step to solving them. If a student's problems are minor (a couple of missing assignments, some disengagement, and so on), I address them with the student first and keep the family informed of this plan. This supports the teacher-student trust that you worked so hard to build. If a problem persists, let students know you're contacting their family out of concern and so that they can help. In the spirit of partnership, clue the family in as a proactive stance: "Your child and I have discussed . . . are working on . . . making progress toward . . . so I wanted to let you know . . ." This way, the partnership stance is established at the beginning of the situation and productive unity is clear.

Let me share an example of how working together proactively can result in stronger relationships between home and school. I was a new teacher when I discovered what my colleagues and I labeled "Senioritis, Eighth Grade Edition." After March, it's very common for eighth graders to become complacent as they look ahead to high school. They're done with the present, forgetful of the past, and eager for the future. As an eighth grade teacher, I learned to predict questions I might be asked and prompt families about these common developmental situations:

- Disengagement from current academic needs that no longer feel like priorities

- Quickly shifting emotions, especially of sadness and nostalgia, as eighth graders start to think about the end of crucial friendships and their journey together

- Anxiety about starting a new school and going to a different school from their friends

- Worry, frustration, and disappointment about whether the next school is the one they wanted (private versus public, or placement based on district boundaries)

This pregraduation time is a whirlwind of celebration and disappointment. As a parent, I remember this stage well. There was the briefest of moments when I thought, "Great! My child just turned a corner and is on their way! Best. Parent. Ever." And then the developmental whiplash came back to hit me hard. However, I was able to learn from this experience and share it with families in my classes. They needed to hear what was normal and what might need additional attention. In my case, I found it helpful to reflect on the developmental basics so I could translate this experience into becoming a better middle school teacher (and a more realistic parent). Two steps forward, one step back is a common developmental occurrence that will show itself again and again with our students. With the right amount of preparation, we can all better face this adventure of eighth grade spring!

Problem-Solve as Partners

We are all unique, and that's to be celebrated. Just as our students have many different layers to their personality and many different cultural backgrounds, so do their families. The positive relationship we established earlier in the year truly helps if and when we ever need to have the hard conversations later. Recently, a new teacher approached me for help with a challenging parent who had asked them, "Why aren't you doing the same thing as the other teachers?" There is the very real possibility this parent was simply anxious or just needed to feel heard, but it's easy to take it personally as an educator when you receive messages like this one. I always take a step back and look at issues like this through a variety of lenses. I advised the teacher to use the information she obtained about the student and family earlier in the year and focus on a few things:

- **Stick with the facts.** It is easier initially to address data than emotions. Start with the facts and move on from there.

- **Stay calm and neutral.** Parents' questions and challenges often mask defensiveness, anxiety, and fear. They may just need validation. Be their safe space and model respect.

- **Express authentic caring.** The best way to get a family on the same page is to show you see, care about, and want the best outcome for their child. It's that simple.

- **Establish an expectation of partnership.** Rather than present yourself as the expert, it's more productive to get the parents' ideas and approach the solution as a united team. You each have insights to offer, and you're stronger on the same team than on competing ones.

In this case, the parent just wanted to make sure important material was covered. When we avoid a reaction and enter these situations with the spirit of collaboration, we see situations from another's perspective. This pays back in ways that can only benefit the student. To extend that connection, in our school we've invited families to contribute as expert presenters, project advisors, or small-group facilitators. Families' experiences are to be respected and valued in the classroom. Often, a little effort to involve them in the classroom will help them see how the eighth grade year supports a successful transition to high school and beyond. It's all about seeing our eighth grade learning as a living, breathing curriculum that is responsive to the students, their families, and the world around them.

Culturally Responsive Teaching Includes Families

A few months ago, I had an "aha" moment while attending a webinar. The presenters discussed ways to include all cultural groups in our classrooms. While we may feel that family-based school support groups should include all our students' parents, the presenters discussed the success their school has had with hosting two types of family groups: cultural-specific and mixed. They found that there was greater family engagement when groups first had a safe space to speak their language and express their thoughts without what they perceived as judgment. They then were more likely to engage with the rest of the class's family community. With both these options, they were better able to contribute to the larger community with a clearer mind—and heart.

Cultural Translation Requires a Different Language

One routine I use during our Responsive Advisory Meeting is greeting in multiple languages. While this may seem like a simple, basic activity, I use it to add an extra level of connection and awareness so students realize everyone has something to contribute. A few years ago, I had a family from Sierra Leone join our class. They arrived from a traumatic situation and were understandably closed off. In building a relationship with them, I started slowly, asking, "How do you say 'hello' to a friend in Sierra Leone?" After taking time to think about it, the man's face lit up with a huge smile as he told me, "Ahhh . . . Kushe!" and took the time to teach me how to pronounce it ("koo-shay"). It also helped the new student see something of value they had to share. It was a small, yet magical, moment. While it takes time to learn and use these words and phrases, it honors those families . . . and rewards us as well.

Small moments like the one above are important steps in helping students, and their families, feel seen and understood. Connecting with a student individually in this way can be scaled up to meet the need of communicating effectively with all families. I'm a naturally effusive communicator; I tend to add details, frame things in the positive, and explain the reasoning to families. While I felt like my communication methods were clear and illustrative, I found that I was not always understood by the parents I partnered with. What I eventually discovered is that I needed to take time to research the ways the different cultures in my class communicate. I worked so hard to frame the message carefully that the meaning of my words was sometimes missed. Cultural and language considerations meant that I needed to be more clear with my communication; I needed to mean what I said and say what I meant.

At the same time, I also learned to be less directive and more collaborative. If I travel to another country (or even a different part of the United States), there are words, phrases, practices, and customs that are essential to efficient and productive communication. It's the same for our families. When I adjust what may seem like seemingly minor details—tone of voice, word choice, or the gestures I use—it helps me to build a bridge between the past and present experiences of my students' families, enabling us to hear what each other has to say.

An eye-opener for me in this area came from our school custodian. I asked her for some quick help translating with a student. Afterward, she let me know some subtle details that helped her do a better job as translator—namely, where exactly the family was from and how long they had been in our community. It guided her in knowing what vocabulary and approach to use with the child and family. I called the custodian my "cultural translator." It helps if you can find a resource like her, even if it means contacting local community organizations, internet sites, or libraries for information. Her expertise helped me adjust the communication I needed to use with this specific family. When I spoke with the parents, "Julio needs to figure out how he's getting to school" became "Can you please do me a favor and go over options with Julio to get to school?" When I spoke to Julio, "When you use language like that to another person, their feelings are hurt and your message is lost" became "Talking like that about someone is mean." Being aware of these additional socio-emotional layers added depth to my relationship with this particular family and created a collaborative partnership that supported the student.

There is so much to learn about our students, their families, and their cultures. Experience and information gained through the family survey we send out at the beginning of the school year is indispensable. Combined with observation and interactions (and sometimes a little detective work), it all provides valuable background information. The best approach I've found is asking questions—lots of questions. I like to start slow and add a deeper level once the connection is made. Here are some questions I ask as I am getting to know families:

- "How can I make _____?" (Food always provides good gateway questions!)
- "How is your holiday celebrated? What's the right greeting?"

- "What are the priorities for raising children in your culture?" (Is it important for them to be well behaved, to have an attractive appearance, to achieve academic success, to have a happy childhood?)
- "What is your expectation for school discipline?"

Final Word

Along with listening to the answers families offer to these questions, I pay close attention to the unspoken ways families and students respond to them. If I sense any discomfort or confusion, I assure them that I am here to learn from them as much as their child is here to learn from me. That's the essence of the partnership between school and home and between teachers and parents. When the adults all learn from each other, the students benefit. When I can meet families on their level first, we can build a relationship and add essential information to create mutual understanding. Meet your students and their families where they are. You'll all be better for it.

Chapter 6
Healthy Teachers, Healthy Classrooms

Overview

In the first five chapters of this book, we discussed significant topics in the field of education: how to respond to students' developmental needs, manage classrooms effectively, build positive communities, engage students in meaningful academics, and connect with families to support students' success. We know from experience and from research that these five areas are crucial for teaching and learning, and taken together, they create classrooms where all students feel safety, significance, and a sense of belonging—just what they need to make academic, social, and emotional progress and find success in the classroom and beyond. But there is one element of education that we haven't mentioned yet, and while it's by far one of the most impactful areas of any educational setting, it's often given the least amount of time (if any time at all) in teacher preparation programs, professional development, school schedules, and more: teacher health and well-being.

Everyone should take steps to support their own health and well-being, but it's a particularly important habit for people in high-stress professions. In a Gallup poll on occupational stress, teachers and nurses tied for the highest reported levels of daily stress (Gallup 2014)—and that was before the toll of the COVID-19 pandemic in 2020 and 2021. While the pandemic changed and complicated teachers' experiences in many stressful ways, it's important to remember that the teaching profession has always had its challenges. According to a 2017 survey from the American Federation of

Teachers and the Badass Teachers Association, 61 percent of teachers described their daily work as often or always stressful.

What Is Stress?

Lisa Dewey Wells, coauthor of *Empowering Educators*, grades K, 1, 2

Stress is the body's way of responding to anything that requires our attention or action, including physical, psychological, or emotional strain. The human body has a two-part nervous system, the sympathetic and parasympathetic systems, that help us respond to stress.

The sympathetic system's job is to help us respond quickly to danger, such as an approaching lion or a child who darts across the street to get a ball as we're driving. This system allows our bodies to rev up, gather energy, and respond quickly, and it also makes us sweat, breathe quickly, and then sometimes have that shaky feeling when the threat dissipates. The parasympathetic system helps our body rest and digest. It calms our breathing, heart rate, and mind. It lets us process information and emotions and restores a sense of calm.

Stress itself has benefits as well as drawbacks. Good stress, called eustress, can help us be more creative and productive and even boost our mood. Bad stress can be overwhelming and often makes it hard to handle the situation at hand. It's important to have time to reflect on stressors and how you handle them. Take a moment to jot down a few of your current stressors. Naming our stressors can help us begin to identify if they create good stress or bad stress and then choose how we want to respond and manage these stressors.

So what is it that makes teaching so stressful? While there are different factors at play for everyone, common themes for many educators include the amount of time and effort they dedicate to their work—far more than forty hours a week (Diliberti, Schwartz, and Grant 2021)—and how effective they feel they are able to be within their classrooms, schools, and districts. Educators are deeply invested in their work and in seeing their students succeed, and feeling ineffective is a significant source of stress and worry among teachers.

Stressing Student Success

Teachers' remarkable dedication to their work and their deep desire to make a difference in students' lives are two of the causes of educator stress. It's a vicious cycle: teachers work so hard to support their students that they can become burned out, which in turn makes them less effective in the classroom, so they need to work even harder! According to Jones and Bouffard (2012), teachers who have strong social and emotional competence themselves are better able to build positive relationships with students, manage their classrooms successfully, and teach social and emotional learning skills effectively. That means that educators dedicated to meeting their students' needs and helping them succeed may find the most success by starting with themselves. In order to be an effective educator, you need to find ways to support your own social and emotional needs. Healthy teachers make healthy classrooms!

In addition to educators' own social and emotional learning skills, there's another powerful, teacher-focused element that contributes to student success. Collective teacher efficacy, or teachers' mutual belief that they are successful in their shared work in their school, is the most significant factor influencing student achievement. Collective efficacy has more than three times the impact and ability to predict student success than socio-economic status, home environment, or student motivation (Hattie 2016). That's remarkable to think about: a group of educators who share a strong belief in the collective work they do in their school can make more of a difference in student success than even the students' own motivation or home life! There is real power in shared teacher beliefs and in the community that teachers find with their colleagues.

These studies about the impact teachers have on students may come as no surprise to you. Anyone who has seen the progress that students make over the course of a school year, the way that educators collaborate to create meaningful learning experiences, and the challenges that both students and teachers can overcome together won't bat an eye at these findings. The powerful impact teachers make doesn't happen magically; it comes from deep commitment, tireless effort, and ceaseless collaboration.

This work takes a toll, and so it's worth restating two important points: healthy teachers make healthy classrooms, and no one can do it alone.

In this chapter, we'll delve into:

- What it means to be a socially and emotionally healthy educator.
- How you can become a strong leader in your classroom and beyond.
- Why it's important to understand your implicit beliefs.
- How you can keep growing and learning as a teacher, colleague, and leader.
- How to take care of yourself so you can take care of your students.

Adult Social and Emotional Learning

In Chapter 1, we discussed developmentally responsive teaching and the four principles of adolescent development. Social and emotional development adheres to those same principles, following a reasonably predictable pattern that individuals progress through at their own pace and at a varying rate over the course of their lives. Social and emotional growth, like all human development, is uneven. There are periods of intense growth and change followed by relatively quiet periods, a spiraling pattern that continues throughout our lifetimes.

That last part is the key, and it's a fact that is often forgotten: human development continues throughout adulthood! Social and emotional growth, in particular, lasts for a lifetime, with readiness to demonstrate social and emotional skills influenced by a variety of circumstances, including sociocultural and economic factors as well as individual personality and experiences.

Lifelong Social and Emotional Learning

These truths about social and emotional development mean that it's possible, and important, for adults to continue learning and demonstrating new social and emotional skills. How many times have you used the phrase "lifelong learner" as an educator? Effective teachers are often the most committed learners, deeply curious about the subjects they teach and the best ways to reach their students. You've probably been focused on your own social and emotional growth throughout your life without even realizing it. Have you ever intentionally focused on being effective while working with others, standing up for yourself, taking responsibility for something in your community, listening and caring for others, or persevering through a difficult time? You've been honing your social and emotional competence throughout all of those actions and more.

Everyone relies on social and emotional skills to be successful in life. Teaching is a deeply social and emotional profession, so it requires educators to call on those skills every minute of every day. The emphasis on these two types of skills is another reason why professions like teaching can be so exhausting and stressful at times; it takes a toll not only on your physical and cognitive energy but also on your social and emotional energy. When you understand more about your social and emotional strengths and tendencies, you are better able to develop the skills you need to be calm, focused, successful, and happy.

> **Social Competence and Emotional Competence**
>
> Social and emotional learning is often talked about as if it's one idea, but there are two crucial parts: social competence and emotional competence. *Social competence* is the ability to make positive contributions to the community and society and to cooperate well with others; it encompasses interpersonal skills like relating to others. *Emotional competence* is the ability to understand your emotions and how those emotions impact the way you feel, think, and act; it encompasses intrapersonal skills like managing your emotions.

Developing Social and Emotional Learning Skills

While that goal may sound lofty, it's possible for anyone to achieve. Like any skill, social and emotional skills can be explicitly taught and intentionally learned. It takes time, practice, and patience to improve your skills, but it makes a difference, not just in your own life, but in the lives of the people around you, from your family to your colleagues to your students. If we don't model, live by, and believe what we say, nothing will change for our students. We know that social and emotional skills are crucial for our students, and they are just as important for us.

Just as we would do with our students' learning, when we focus on our own learning, it's helpful to start with a sense of the skills and competencies we aim to develop. Over time, there have been many different definitions and terms applied to these skills and competencies. Two organizations that have been committed for decades to bringing social and emotional learning to the forefront of education are Center for Responsive Schools, founded in 1981, and the Collaborative for Academic, Social, and Emotional Learning (CASEL), founded in 1994. Both organizations have identified five core social and emotional learning competencies, and while the two organizations use different terms to describe these competencies, the terms correspond closely to each other.

The chart that follow provides definitions of each of the terms and shows how the Center for Responsive Schools competencies (in the left-hand column) and the CASEL competencies (in the right-hand column) connect to each other. In the center column are anchor standards that connect to each one of the Center for Responsive Schools competencies. These standards encompass the abilities an individual needs to exhibit to successfully demonstrate social and emotional competence. They provide a solid grounding for considering learning goals for your students as well as yourself.

C.A.R.E.S.		CASEL
Competencies	Anchor Standards	Core Competencies
Cooperation The ability to establish new relationships, to maintain positive relationships and friendships, to avoid social isolation, to resolve conflicts, to accept differences, and to be a contributing member of the classroom and community in which one lives, works, learns, and plays	• Able to make and keep friends • Works with others toward a common goal • Resolves differences quickly • Cooperates as a group leader or a member of the group • Exhibits helpfulness	**Relationship Skills** The abilities to establish and maintain healthy and supportive relationships and to effectively navigate settings with diverse individuals and groups
Assertiveness The ability to take initiative, to stand up for one's ideas without hurting or negating others, to seek help, to persevere with a challenging task, and to recognize one's individual self as separate from the environment, circumstances, or conditions one is in	• Expresses strong emotions and opinions effectively • Able to seek help • Shows openness and honesty • Persists through challenging events • Takes the initiative to do what is right, fair, and just • Makes choices one feels good about later	**Self-Awareness** The abilities to understand one's own emotions, thoughts, and values and how they influence behavior across contexts
Responsibility The ability to motivate oneself to act and follow through on expectations; to define a problem, consider the consequences, and choose a positive solution	• Selects the best option among choices for a suitable outcome • Holds oneself accountable • Demonstrates social, civic, and digital responsibility • Takes care of property	**Responsible Decision-Making** The abilities to make caring and constructive choices about personal behavior and social interactions across diverse situations
Empathy The ability to recognize, appreciate, or understand another's state of mind or emotions; to be receptive to new ideas and perspectives; and to see, appreciate, and value differences and diversity in others	• Recognizes and manages one's own emotions and recognizes the emotions of others • Respects and values diversity in others • Respects differing cultural norms • Aware of the impact of one's actions on others	**Social Awareness** The abilities to understand the perspectives of and empathize with others, including those from diverse backgrounds, cultures, and contexts
Self-Control The ability to recognize and regulate one's thoughts, emotions, and behaviors in order to be successful in the moment and remain on a successful trajectory	• Adheres to social, behavioral, and moral standards • Manages overwhelming thoughts or emotions • Controls impulses and delays gratification • Shows hope and perseverance	**Self-Management** The abilities to manage one's emotions, thoughts, and behaviors effectively in different situations and to achieve goals and aspirations

Demonstrating Readiness

As you read the anchor standards listed in the chart, you might have found yourself pausing on certain skills and thinking, "I do this most of the time, but not all the time." For instance, you might usually work well with others toward a common goal, but if your strong feeling about how to achieve that goal clashes with someone else's, you might choose to stand your ground. Maybe you make choices you feel good about most of the time, but every so often, there's something you regret in hindsight. That just means you're human! This back and forth is all part of social and emotional learning.

There is no such thing as complete mastery of social and emotional skills. No one can make the right choice all the time, or resolve every single difference quickly, or show hope and perseverance every minute of every day. But we can strive for readiness to demonstrate these skills most of the time, and we can learn more about ourselves and deepen our skills when we encounter moments that challenge us.

Learning About Yourself

It's also important to emphasize that developing social and emotional competence means coming to understand yourself and the ways you tend to feel, think, and behave. There is no one right way to demonstrate the core social and emotional competencies of cooperation, assertiveness, responsibility, empathy, and self-control. There are many possible ways to be assertive, for instance; some ways work for certain people or in certain situations, but not in others. Understanding your social and emotional tendencies—the way you usually approach situations involving these competencies—can help you manage your emotions, thoughts, and behaviors.

One way to think about your tendencies is to consider your own range of possible reactions within the competencies. Each of the five social and emotional learning competencies encompasses a spectrum of behaviors. At the end of each spectrum are two dichotomous sets of behavioral tendencies for demonstrating social and emotional competence. Within each spectrum, there are many variations and possibilities. For example, under the social and emotional competency of cooperation, at one end of the spectrum we have the Synergist, whose tendency is to be highly collaborative, and at the other end we have the Insulator, who will engage in group work if invited but whose tendency is to view people's roles separately rather than collectively. Each of the dichotomies, and the variations in between, can represent a meaningful and valid way to behave and to react in academic and social settings. The key for us as teachers is to understand where our tendencies lie within this spectrum.

> ### Understanding Your Social and Emotional Type
> The dichotomies for each of the five social and emotional learning competencies were developed through research done at Center for Responsive Schools as part of the development of Fly Five, a social and emotional learning curriculum for kindergarten through eighth grade. Part of the Fly Five program includes the Social and Emotional Type Inventory, a typological assessment for adults to help educators better understand their own social and emotional competence as they teach social and emotional learning skills to their students. Scan this QR code for more information about Fly Five.

As your social and emotional skills grow and change over the course of your life, where you fall along each continuum can and will shift. Take a look at the traits for each dichotomy in the five social and emotional learning competencies to get a sense of your tendencies.

C.A.R.E.S. Competency Traits

Cooperation

Synergists:

- Are highly collaborative and want to hear all ideas and suggestions.
- Are quick to help resolve conflicts.
- Develop long and lasting friendships.
- Are highly collaborative no matter the situation.

Insulators:

- Engage meaningfully in group work when there is a clear benefit to it.
- Consider everyone's role separately rather than collectively.
- Are not interested in conflicts, either resolving them or starting them.
- Develop shorter, intense friendships.

Assertiveness

Expectors:

- Express their ideas, feelings, and emotions clearly while acknowledging those of others.
- Are usually open to receiving help or feedback.
- Are confident in their ability to succeed at new or challenging tasks.

Hypothesizers:

- Carefully analyze situations.
- Can sometimes hesitate to express their own ideas, feelings, and emotions for fear of hurting others.
- Are quick to think for others, but tend to doubt themselves.
- Don't always trust others to do things, so they take on extra responsibility themselves.

Responsibility

Navigators:

- Are intrinsically motivated as they want to be seen as trustworthy and dependable.
- Work hard to manage their emotions in order to modify their behavior and consider the consequences of their actions in order to best align with expectations.
- Tend to be careful and consistent.

Traversers:

- Rely on extrinsic cues, prompts, and reminders to help them make good choices.
- Often make decisions by choosing a preferred option, which can sometimes lead to unforeseen consequences.
- Tend to be spontaneous and impulsive.

Empathy	
Associates:	Limiters:
• Can read and understand the emotions and behaviors of others. • Value the diverse perspectives they gain from connecting with others. • Consistently act on their feelings of empathy to care for others.	• Make decisions based on their own feelings and emotions. • Do not always consider the impact of their actions on others. • Show compassion and caring for those similar to themselves but do not always extend that empathy to those who are significantly different.

Self-Control	
Regulators:	Adventurers:
• Like to be in control. • Hold themselves to high standards. • Are motivated to see their goals through to the end. • Use their willpower and confidence to stay hopeful and persevere through difficulties.	• Do things differently and think outside the box. • Live in the moment without thinking about the consequences of their actions. • Seek strategies, resources, and help outside of themselves to solve problems.

Cooperation, assertiveness, responsibility, empathy, and self-control are vital skills for everyone, especially those in professions like education that require strong social and emotional skills. As teachers, we connect with a wide range of colleagues, families, and students all day every day, and inevitably, we find ourselves in situations with people who react differently than we do. Recognizing our own social and emotional tendencies and those of the people around us can help us better understand ourselves and others.

Imagine, for instance, that you tend toward the Regulator end of the self-control spectrum and like to plan in advance and stay in control of a situation, and you work with a grade-level partner who tends to be more of an Adventurer, someone who spontaneously changes direction and is guided by what's happening in the moment. How would you approach that partnership compared to one with another Regulator? What challenges would that pairing present, and what strengths would it bring forward? Now imagine that you tend to be more of an Expector in the realm of assertiveness; you are eager to try new approaches and thrive on immediate feedback. Your supervisor is more of a Hypothesizer, someone who meticulously reviews a situation before responding and is tentative about delegating. How would your awareness of your own approach and your supervisor's approach change how you might assert yourself in this situation?

Growing Pains

Linda Berger

Recently, I led a four-day workshop at a middle school with a primarily Black student population and a primarily white teaching staff. The workshop took place at the end of the school year, at a time when the educators were exhausted from a demanding year yet deeply committed to returning in the fall with a renewed passion for equity and relationships.

Our discussions often revolved around how to foster authentic connections with students who desperately need and want to be seen. How can we reach students with academic challenges that reflect not only the reality our students live in but also their aspirations for the future? Where can we find meaningful, culturally responsive materials to teach the required curriculum? Does our teaching truly come from a place of empathy and understanding?

As we questioned our beliefs, our practices, and our resources together, we recognized that we all have room to grow. That knowledge can be uncomfortable. But when growth comes from a place of true compassion, the results elevate us all and help create a better world for our students.

As you consider your own social and emotional competence and grow more aware of the skills and tendencies you recognize in the people around you, it's important to keep in mind that there are no right or wrong reactions to emotions. There is no one way that you, or the people you encounter, should feel. Developing your skills in and understanding of the C.A.R.E.S. competencies allows you to gain insight into how you feel, how others might be feeling, and how you can respond to those emotions so that you stay on a successful path.

Final Word

Awareness of your social and emotional strengths and areas for growth is the first step in developing skills in social and emotional competence. As you become more aware of your emotions, thoughts, and behaviors, you can embark on your own natural learning cycle and learn more, set goals, practice skills, and continue your social and emotional development.

Teacher Leadership

Teachers wear many hats: instructor, coach, cheerleader, referee, entertainer, mentor, and so much more. A particularly important role is that of leader. You might think of yourself as a leader in your classroom, but it's important to remember the leadership role you occupy in other areas as well. As educators, we usually think of ourselves in relation to our students, but we are also part of a crucial community of adults within our school. How we work together as adults to create a safe, joyful, and inclusive environment is as important as our individual contributions or competence. No matter how effective an educator you are within the walls of your classroom, the environment outside your classroom is just as important for your students. It's vital that we work together with other adults in our school, in our students' families, and in our community to support student success. You are not just a leader among your students; you are a leader for your students.

Understanding yourself as a leader starts with thinking about your leadership style. Your teacher leadership style impacts the community you build in your classroom, how you manage your classroom, and how you relate to others, including your students, their families, and your colleagues. Think back to the C.A.R.E.S. competencies and dichotomies we were just discussing. The way you firmly yet fairly understand, manage, and balance your classroom community connects with every one of the five social and emotional competencies. The professional way you conduct yourself with your students, their families, and your colleagues sends an important message about who you are as a leader and your implicit beliefs about students and their potential.

What we say and how we say it are also part of who we are as leaders. Our words reveal what we believe. We all have implicit beliefs and biases that we have to learn to recognize, and the words we choose can give light to those implicit beliefs. We've talked a lot in this book about teacher language and how powerful our words are. Your leadership style is reflected in what you say and also in how you act, two crucial aspects of effective classroom management and behavior management. Your approach to discipline comes out of your leadership style. Your words and actions are impactful outside the classroom, too, and they send important messages to the adults in your community about who you are and what you believe. Thinking about your current leadership style and how to grow to become the type of teacher leader you want to be can also help you clarify your beliefs and approach to teaching and learning.

Leading In and Out of the Classroom

Amanda Stessen-Blevins, coauthor of *Empowering Educators*, grades 3, 4, 5

Recently, I was in an adult meeting in which people were talking over each other, making it difficult to hear the ideas of those trying to share. Frequently, the loudest person kept interrupting and bulldozing over everyone else's ideas until they were the only one speaking. We've all probably been in a meeting like this at one point or another; it's unproductive and incredibly frustrating.

In this particular meeting, it suddenly occurred to me that had this behavior occurred in a classroom setting where I was the teacher, it would have played out very differently:

- I would have stepped in to make the space safer for all voices to be heard. I would have authoritatively supported students to take turns talking if students were not yet able to do that themselves.

- I would have supported students who were learning to be more assertive by asking, "Could you say more about that, _____? It didn't sound like you were finished sharing your idea."

- For students having difficulty leaving space for others' ideas, I would encourage their developing skills in self-control, empathy, and cooperation by reminding them of our classroom norms, incorporating visual cues to activate their listening skills, and using redirecting language to guide their behavior.

- In my role as the teacher, I would have scanned the space and challenged my implicit biases, asking myself, "Are there voices that have been heard more than others? Do I observe anyone who looks like they want to say something but hasn't yet?"

As I was processing my realization of how differently I would have managed the situation with children compared to adults, I had to ask myself some challenging questions: "Why do I feel more comfortable supporting students with this common conflict? Why don't I feel comfortable to assert myself in the same way when I'm in a meeting with adults?" I realized that the same skills I teach my students and strive to model in the classroom are also strategies I can apply outside of the classroom with family, friends, and yes, even with colleagues in a professional meeting. Just as we support students with curiosity and compassion, we must give the same grace to ourselves and our own learning.

The following leadership styles represent broad categories of what teacher leaders can look like in a classroom. While the styles are described from a classroom perspective, imagine how it might feel to work with someone who models each of these styles. What type of colleague would you prefer to work with?

Teacher Leadership Styles

	Autocratic	Permissive	Flip-Flop	Authoritative
Sounds like . . .	"Because I said so."	"Can you please cooperate now?"	"I said no. Okay, one more chance. This time I mean it! Actually . . ."	"Let me show you . . ."
Looks like . . .	The teacher tends to rely on external means—punishments and rewards—to get students to behave.	The teacher tends to rely on ignoring and bargaining to keep students happy.	The teacher bounces back and forth between autocratic and permissive approaches.	The teacher uses strategies like Interactive Modeling, teacher language, and logical consequences to shape positive behaviors.
Sends the message that . . .	Children are naturally unruly and impulsive, requiring strict rules to keep them quiet and obedient.	The most important thing is to be liked, which is achieved by being nice, offering praise, and ignoring undesirable actions.	The teacher's reactions are inconsistent, and it's not clear to students what the expectations are.	The teacher believes students want to do what's right and supports that goal with clear guidance and expectations.
Leads to students feeling . . .	Anxious, angry, and resentful.	Tense, unsure, and emotionally unsafe.	Confused, frustrated, and anxious.	Empowered, confident, and successful.

Final Word

You may recognize the authoritative leadership style as the one we have described throughout this book: firm, fair, professional, respectful, kind, and empathetic. Just as social and emotional growth takes time, so does growing as a leader. Being aware of the message your words and actions send is the first step to becoming an authoritative leader. The second is coaching yourself when you make a mistake and rehearsing alternative choices. Your leadership style is an important tool for your work with students and adults alike. As you become aware of your current leadership approach and set goals for developing your authoritative approach, you will have opportunities to consider what you believe about education and how your words and actions can support those beliefs.

Power of Teacher Beliefs

Our individual and collective beliefs have a huge impact on our work in schools and our effectiveness as educators. When our beliefs are conscious and healthy, like the collective belief in teacher efficacy described in the overview of this chapter, then the results are often positive and productive ones, such as improved academic outcomes for students and high morale for teachers. But we all have implicit biases, attitudes, or stereotypes we hold outside of our conscious awareness. Those implicit biases can get in the way of our conscious dedication to equity in education and impact our words, emotions, and actions.

Extensive research, particularly in K–12 school settings, has shown that implicit bias has a significant impact on discipline in schools, perceptions of behavior, and even teaching practices and leadership styles (Kirwan Institute for the Study of Race and Ethnicity 2018). It's crucial for educators to recognize their individual beliefs and biases, but the work doesn't stop there. The next step is to consciously let go of biases and of the beliefs that do not serve educators or students well, and cultivate or hold on to beliefs that are beneficial.

Identifying Implicit Biases

A first step is bringing awareness to implicit biases by intentionally pausing and asking yourself questions to get below the surface of your actions and words (Kirwan Institute for the Study of Race and Ethnicity 2018). Three simple questions, recommended by the National Education Association (n.d.), that you can ask yourself are:

1. What is true for you? Consider what past experiences you've had that you may carry with you.

2. What do you value? Think about what's most important to you and identify what your priorities are.

3. What's your privilege? Bring your awareness to the advantages you have had in your experience that others have not.

Another step in growing your awareness of implicit or unconscious biases is to explore an implicit association test, or IAT, like the ones developed by psychologists at Harvard University, the University of Virginia, and the University of Washington at Project Implicit (Project Implicit 2011). These IATs examine the link between hidden biases and observable behavior. There are several IATs available through Project Implicit that measure implicit associations about a wide range of topics. The IATs are available for free and may be taken easily online. These tests may not provide all of the nuanced data that an individualized, in-person assessment might offer, but they do give useful initial insights into biases you may not have been aware of. As you explore your own beliefs and biases, you can build your awareness and work on changing your beliefs through practices like mindfulness to build empathy for those with different perspectives and building connections with people who are different from you (Kirwan Institute for the Study of Race and Ethnicity 2018).

As you bring your focus to your implicit beliefs, you can also think about your explicit beliefs and ensure that they serve you and your students well. Some beliefs contribute to our collective efficacy and to students' growing social and emotional learning skills. Those are beliefs we want to embrace, develop, and share with others. Shared teacher beliefs don't develop overnight, but they improve through strong instructional leadership and consistent opportunities for teacher collaboration, like structured professional learning and opportunities to observe colleagues. In turn, these shared beliefs can lead to improved student achievement (Goddard et al. 2015).

Putting Student Behavior Into Perspective

Brian Smith

Often, teachers are the first adults that students see each day besides their family members. Sometimes, they may see their teachers even more than certain family members! Young people will often lash out at the ones closest to them, and so we often find ourselves at the center of a young person's life when they need to vent. This behavior can be hurtful and feel personal, but it's important to remind yourself that student behavior usually has very little to do with your classroom or your teaching. Most of the time, in fact, students are often not even aware of the impact their behavior has on their teachers or others around them.

The sooner we realize that we are not the target of student behavior, even if it appears that way, the sooner we are able to get students the help and support they need. Keep these tips in mind:

- **Stay calm.** We must maintain a professional and kind front no matter how a student behaves.
- **Remind them you care.** When the student is ready, take a quiet moment one-on-one to talk and determine how you can help them.
- **Use your resources.** If you feel overwhelmed by the situation, take the student to another adult who can offer a fresh perspective.
- **Be firm yet kind.** Our students rely on us for a stable and consistent environment. Once a student has calmed down, they should be able to rejoin the class and maintain their sense of belonging in the classroom community.

Teacher Beliefs That Promote Social and Emotional Learning

Teacher beliefs are a set of principles, assumptions, values, and convictions that educators hold true regarding students, the classroom, education and educational concepts, curriculum, pedagogy, and discipline. This belief system guides and informs their thoughts, actions, and classroom behaviors, forms the basis for decision-making, and helps to sort, organize, and prioritize information. Center for Responsive Schools has identified eight teacher belief domains that are critical to teachers' approach to education. These eight domains lie at the heart of social and emotional learning in the classroom and the school.

Conditions for Learning	Belief that students learn best in environments of high expectations that are student centered, developmentally responsive, academically challenging, and safe to make learning mistakes.
Conditions for Effective Teaching	Belief that teaching is most effective when lessons are planned and designed with knowledge of students, including evidence-based practices and strategies, and offer learning goals and instructional activities that are directly related to expectations for what a student should know and be able to do at the end of the instructional chunk.
Goal of Discipline	Belief that the goal of discipline is to teach students to be in control of themselves and to choose socially and morally responsible behavior because it is the right thing to do, not because of fear of punishment or hope of reward. Belief that teaching students self-discipline and self-control develops goal-setting, problem-solving, and critical thinking skills and helps them to become good citizens who exhibit pro-social behaviors and demonstrate respect for self, others, and property.
Goodness of Student Intentions	Belief that educators should hold and communicate positive beliefs and expectations for all students, including those who may have different values than they do; are culturally, racially, or socioeconomically different from them; who appear disengaged and unmotivated; or who struggle and misbehave. Belief that problem behaviors result from unmet needs or lack of skills rather than the student's character, family background, or intention to do harm.

Nature of Learning	Belief that learning is cognitively constructed and relies on social, emotional, and cooperative processes. Belief that learning builds on prior knowledge, is facilitated through choice and through understanding of students' context and interests, and becomes transferrable to a new context when there is an emphasis on process as well as outcome. Belief that changes in the learner happen because of the learning experience.
Purpose of Education	Belief that the purpose of education is to build in students a social consciousness and a strong sense of self, to cultivate the attitudes and dispositions of good citizenship, and to teach students to participate in the democratic process. Belief that education should provide new experiences and open windows for students to see and pursue a bright future for themselves, their families, and their local and global communities. Belief that the purpose of education is to enable students to read, speak, write, and listen well; to work well with numbers and technology; to think, reason, wonder, and be curious; to appreciate and value music, art, culture, movement, and athletics; and to manage themselves and know how to cooperate well with others.
Role of Social and Emotional Skills in Learning	Belief that the social and emotional curriculum has equal weight as the core academic curriculum and that social and emotional learning includes (a) school and classroom environments that support the development of social and emotional learning skills and (b) time and resources given for explicit instruction in social and emotional skill development.
Role of School and Classroom Environment	Belief that the school and classroom are a community in which all students belong, can operate autonomously and responsibly, and feel represented, welcome, and accepted as members of the school and academic community.

Imagine the power of a school community in which all educators consciously share these eight powerful beliefs and strive to ensure that their words and actions align with those beliefs. That kind of community would need to commit to continued exploration, collaboration, and reflection—an ongoing learning cycle that supports these shared beliefs and the teachers who hold them.

> ### Building Shared Beliefs
> Collective efficacy doesn't happen overnight. It's something school communities have to work toward and constantly fine-tune. You might find yourself in a school community where you have a different mindset or belief system from those around you. Feeling alone or different from your colleagues can be frustrating and discouraging. How do you create a community of colleagues from the ground up? Start by making a connection with one person from your school. See the next section, "Professional Growth," for ideas that can help build these bonds.

Final Word

Exploring your own implicit biases and beliefs is deeply personal work, and it can have powerful results for you and your students. It's not easy, and it is a particular challenge to address in isolation. Finding colleagues or, even better, a whole school community committed to embracing this work will make it even more engaging and effective. Remember to have empathy for yourself as you go through this reflective process. You will be learning new ways of thinking about the world and your place in it, and there will be moments of discomfort and disquiet. That's an important part of the learning process, and going through it allows us to make stronger, more meaningful connections on the other side. Give yourself the same grace and patience you offer your students. Just like them, you are learning, growing, and changing through this work.

Professional Growth

Whether it's learning more about your students and their families, discovering new books and resources to bring into the classroom, honing instructional approaches, exploring new information in a content area, or finding the answer to a student question, there is always more to learn when it comes to teaching. The most effective teachers are those who are eager to delve more deeply into the art and practice of teaching, and who are always ready to try something new or consider an idea from a new perspective.

In the same way that we encourage our students to take the initiative to ask questions and seek answers, it's important to support our own continued growth and learning. Professional growth feeds your curiosity, challenges your brain, and makes you a better teacher. It's also a great opportunity to model your own learning for your students. Learning more about new approaches can ultimately help you work smarter, not harder! However, with school schedules only getting busier and busier, professional learning is often something many educators put off until another time. So how can you make time to dive more deeply into a topic when your daily schedule barely has time for lunch?

The Gift of Time

Kirsten Lee Howard, coauthor of *Empowering Educators*, grades K, 1, 2

Years ago, my partner and I were brand-new parents to a tiny baby. We were overwhelmed navigating our new life as parents. We'd already figured out how to be full-time working adults, but we suddenly had a tiny person we wanted to spend time with, so staying an hour or two late at work or going out of town for a workshop were no longer attractive options.

One night, as I was trying to get work done at 10:30 p.m. after an evening of family time and rocking the baby to sleep, I lamented, "I just need five full hours to get stuff done!" At first, that seemed like an impossible wish, but the more we talked about it, the more realistic it became. It turned out that if we took time to plan for it, each of us could have one monthly catch-up night.

That night became a gift of time. I worked it out with the administration and the custodial staff at my school so they knew to expect me. Once a month, I'd either order dinner or pack one, say goodbye to my students at dismissal, shut my classroom door, and have several uninterrupted hours to accomplish what I needed to do. Some nights, that meant organizing the space and rotating stations, while other nights, it was deeper learning and planning for the future.

Because I would schedule the time in advance, I could keep a running list of tasks for my catch-up night, which also helped me prioritize valuable time during the school day for planning lessons and making adjustments to the learning my students were doing. It was so freeing to keep a small bin in the classroom for catch-up night and give myself permission to focus on other tasks until then. By the end of the night, I would be exhausted but exhilarated. Walking into the classroom the next morning and seeing all I had accomplished the night before gave me such satisfaction.

In the grand scheme of things, I don't always advocate for teachers spending long nights at school—we often do too much of that—but for me, planning for one long night every four to five weeks gave me a sense of balance. When I was at home, I could focus on my family, and when I was at school, I could use my time fully and well.

When we think about professional growth and development, we often think of formal opportunities like doing graduate work, taking a course or workshop, or participating in schoolwide learning. These options are valid, useful, and interesting, but they also require an investment of time and money that means they are not choices we can make every day. Luckily, there are many other, informal ways to incorporate professional learning and growth into your busy schedule.

You don't need to wait for scheduled professional development days to begin exploring the options available to you for learning and growth. Informal opportunities for professional growth are all around us, from free webinars to meaningful reading material to insightful colleagues. The following are some easily accessible and often free ways to support your own growth as an educator that can work with your schedule and that you can tailor to your particular needs and interests:

- **Find a mentor.** Perhaps, as a new teacher, you were lucky enough to be assigned a mentor teacher—someone to guide you, answer questions, offer advice and insights, bounce ideas off of, and more. If not, don't let that stop you! A professional mentor can be a colleague you have worked with, a match through your college alumni network, a connection you make at a workshop or conference, or even someone you've never met but find through mutual friends, shared interests or experiences, or social media. Wherever they come from, mentors are an invaluable resource for building confidence, offering guidance, and supporting your growth.

- **Observe other classrooms—and welcome observers into your own.** Watching other teachers in action is one of the best ways to learn. You might choose to observe your own students with a special subject teacher, visit the classrooms of colleagues who teach in the grades above and below you, seek out grade-level colleagues, or even observe someone who teaches content completely different from yours. Classroom observations don't have to be long—just ten or fifteen minutes can often be enough. If peer observations aren't already part of your school's routine, you can suggest this practice to your administrator as a free and effective way for colleagues to learn from one another. If you have breaks during your teaching schedule, you might be able to work in an observation or two each term on your own. Most colleagues will be flattered that you are interested in observing them, and they may want the chance to see you in action, as well. It's a great opportunity to discuss your practice with a trusted colleague and learn from their insights.

- **Read, listen, and watch.** There are more amazing books, podcasts, videos, and webinars available to educators now than ever before. Many are free, but many of those that aren't are affordable and worth the investment. Whether it's social and emotional learning, culturally responsive teaching, brain-based strategies, approaches for different content areas, or something else, the resources are robust and readily available. You can read, listen, and watch independently, or find a colleague or two to start an informal book group or discussion to further build on your learning.

- **Think outside the box.** Learning a new skill, delving more deeply into a hobby, or reading about something completely outside of education can inform your teaching in unexpected ways. When you take on the role of the learner rather than the teacher, you have the chance to experience your own natural learning cycle, understand your cognitive approach in different ways, and develop empathy for what your students experience on a daily basis in your classroom. Plus, it's fun to learn something new and to make connections to your prior knowledge and experience.

- **Intentionally seek others' perspectives.** Whether it's on social media or in real life, we can easily find ourselves in a bubble with people who share our viewpoints and backgrounds. Consciously reaching out to people outside that bubble can be an eye-opening experience. A first step toward this goal could be diversifying the media you consume—those you follow on social media, what you watch and listen to—to include new voices and perspectives that could add to your learning.

- **Look at your curriculum through a new lens.** At some point in your planning for the next school year, term, or unit, you will likely take some time to review the lesson plans and student-facing resources that you use in your classroom. That's the perfect moment to look at your lessons and curriculum through a new lens. You might ask yourself:

- "How can I link this content to current events to make real-life connections?"
- "What perspectives are missing from this lesson? Whose stories aren't being told?"
- "Where can I add opportunities for students to engage with each other and learn both actively and interactively?"

- **Create your own professional learning community.** Many schools build professional learning communities, or PLCs, into their annual professional development work. PLCs can be a wonderful way to connect with colleagues and explore resources relevant to your school or district. You can also build your own PLC with colleagues who share interests, goals, and questions that are similar to yours. With so many online resources and connections available, your PLC can be local or global, in person or virtual, and short or long term. Learning alongside other practitioners can be an effective way to add to your teacher toolbox.

- **Set and track professional goals for yourself.** There are so many opportunities for professional learning out there that it's easy to become daunted. Identifying one or two professional goals to focus on each year, and then breaking those goals up into actionable steps, is one way to approach your professional learning. Sharing these goals with a mentor or a PLC can also be an effective way to collaborate on, and stay on top of, achieving these goals.

Final Word

No matter how many years you have been teaching, there is always more to learn. Sometimes it seems like the more you learn, the more you realize there is to learn! Professional learning is also a wonderful way to expand your interests, connect with colleagues all over the globe, and of course, better meet the needs of your students. In addition, the knowledge and resources that come with that learning can go a long way to helping you feel confident, effective, and hopeful in your teaching practice, even when facing a challenge.

• • • • • • • • •

Taking Care of Yourself

Teaching is one of the most challenging and rewarding professions out there. Educators take on and deal with so much each and every day. We stay up late thinking of ways to help struggling students, stay after school planning engaging activities, and spend our free time reading books like this one—all in an effort to be the best teachers we can be for our students.

This work can take a physical and emotional toll, and summer break is simply not enough time to recharge batteries that are fully drained after an intense school year. You know yourself and what you need to be at your best. Think about what you already do to take care of yourself. Are you someone who needs a solid eight hours of sleep every night? Do you need to take a walk every day? A quiet cup of coffee in the morning? A few minutes to unwind with a favorite podcast? Everyone rejuvenates in different ways; what's important is that you find a way that works for you.

What Is Self-Care?

Lisa Dewey Wells, coauthor of *Empowering Educators*, grades K, 1, 2

Self-care tends to get a pretty shiny, exciting, and enticing reputation. But it doesn't have to be about a spa day, massage, or weekend with your best friends (unless that's what works for you!). A simple, practical, and nourishing way to think about self-care revolves around two key elements: it's something you do just for yourself, and it's intentional.

I know a parent who uses dinner prep time to put on headphones and listen to a favorite podcast. For her, that's self-care. I know countless people who get up early to run or swim, and that's their self-care. It doesn't matter what you do to refill your cup and nourish yourself, but devoting just a few minutes each day to intentionally doing something just for you can help strengthen you for the heavy lifting of teaching and caring for others. Self-care can be as simple as:

- Moving (walk, swim, yoga, tennis, dancing)
- Resting (a quick nap in the afternoon or cutting back on binge-watching or social media scrolling to get just a few more minutes of sleep)
- Laughing (alone, with friends, with your students)
- Creating (knitting, building, painting, preparing a meal)
- Breathing (slowly and deeply on your own, with an app, or in a class)
- Connecting (being truly present with just yourself or with someone you care about)

If you're looking for more ideas for self-care routines, the following are some tips we've compiled for practices you can embed in your daily life so that self-care is something you do every day:

- **Take care of your physical body.** Simple things like replacing soda with water, choosing healthy snacks, decreasing your sugar intake, adding more water to your diet, or getting enough sleep can make a huge difference in how you feel physically. When your body feels energized, it has a positive impact on your thoughts and feelings.

- **Talk about it.** It's important and healthy to talk about your thoughts, feelings, and experiences. Think of it like a balloon; if we don't let air out of our balloons by talking about things, eventually we pop. Make and take time to talk to someone (family member, friend, colleague) about your work. Sometimes a colleague who doesn't teach what you teach can be the best sounding board. When you have a trusted relationship, it provides the ability to brainstorm, discuss, and confide, supporting your own emotional well-being. There is also an active and enthusiastic online community of educators on social media platforms that offers valuable connection, support, and ideas no matter where you are. Now more than ever, we're recognizing the part mental health plays in overall wellness. If you're feeling overwhelmed, distressed, or anxious, consider consulting a healthcare professional. Many schools offer employee assistance programs with counseling, and your insurance provider or local community will also have resources. You don't have to go it alone.

- **Look for ways to bring joy to your day.** Even in a job you love, there will be days that are less exciting and happy than others. When those days happen, it is important to have a few strategies to call on to boost yourself up. You might need to step outside to get some fresh air on days that are particularly stressful or run to the local coffee shop during lunch. Maybe you need to set aside a few minutes to do a quick mindfulness exercise. On days that are hard, ask yourself, "What can I do today to take care of myself? What will bring me joy today?"

- **Take brain breaks.** Consider incorporating a fun brain break into your teaching when things feel tense. These activities only take a short time, but often those few minutes of fun and activity are all it takes to bring a smile back to your face. Using this strategy can also be a teachable moment for your students. On a demanding day, for instance, you might say, "I'm noticing that my mind is wandering. I think I need a quick break to refocus and recharge. Let's play Double This, Double That together."

Finding a Healthy Balance

Andy Moral, coauthor of *Empowering Educators*, grades 3, 4, 5

A few school years ago, I struggled with maintaining a healthy balance between my professional life and personal life. Many days, I would come home after a long day feeling exhausted, emotionally drained, and irritable. These feelings, coupled with what seemed like a never-ending to-do list, had me questioning whether I was nearing the point of teacher burnout.

I spent the following summer identifying ways to recalibrate my mental health. With time to recharge and reenergize, I felt great heading into the next school year, but I worried about supporting my well-being as the year progressed. I knew I couldn't wait until summer break to rejuvenate; I needed to dedicate time to taking care of myself throughout the school year and even during the school day. That year, I set a few goals for myself. I tried to:

- **Focus on the five senses.** When you set up your classroom space, be sure to incorporate homey touches that make your workspace a welcoming, comfortable environment. A favorite water bottle, a beautiful plant, or a funny family photo will bring a sense of calm or a smile to your face during the day.

- **Support the need for social interaction.** Teachers share the same needs for social interaction their students have! Connect with teammates and colleagues in your building—have lunch together, join a committee together, or work together on planning a student project.

- **Practice being grateful**. At the end of the school day, maybe before you leave your classroom or during your commute home, identify something you are happy about from that day with students. You could even jot a note about it in your plan book to keep a record of these important moments.

- **Create healthy boundaries.** Be cognizant of the amount of time spent outside the school day working on school tasks. Taking steps like setting a time at night when you no longer check email until the following morning will preserve a healthy separation between home and work.

Incorporating these strategies into my days has helped me stay better calibrated in my professional and personal life. Find out what works best for you to support your well-being, avoid teacher burnout, and be the best teacher that you can be.

- **Put mindfulness on the schedule.** Spending five to ten minutes on taking some deep breaths, doing a short visualization exercise, or taking a quick walk outside can help you refocus and recharge for the rest of the day. You can set aside this time for yourself if you have a scheduled break during the day, but you can also incorporate quick mindfulness exercises into your teaching time, as well. Your students will also benefit from a few minutes to reset as they transition from one class to the next.

- **If you need a break, take a break.** With some preliminary arrangement, you can lean on your colleagues for support and let them lean on you. If you need a break, you can let your colleagues know, and they can step in for you for a moment while you grab a drink of water, make a cup of coffee, or go outside for a few seconds.

- **Notice the positives.** We often focus on the negatives—what didn't go well, what we shouldn't have said—and skip over the positives. There's great benefit to dwelling on those positive moments and reminding ourselves of all the good and growth we witness in our daily work. You can build this practice into your weekly schedule with a routine like jotting down your "wins of the week" (WOW) in your planner to help develop the habit of identifying and reflecting on the positives. Another positive practice is creating a smile file, a place to stash those one-of-a-kind, tug-at-your-heart notes, artwork, and messages from students, families, or even administrators and colleagues. On difficult days, you can pull out your smile file and remember why you do this, that you can do this, and that there are always better days ahead.

- **Step away.** In the evenings and on the weekends, it's easy to be tempted to keep working. There are always lessons to prepare, emails to respond to, and assignments to review. Remember, though, that taking care of yourself so you can be there for your students is what's most important during those off-duty times. Take time to step away so that you can return with renewed strength and perspective.

Focus on Ta-Das, Not To-Dos

Kirsten Lee Howard, coauthor of *Empowering Educators*, grades K, 1, 2

I have a former colleague and good friend with whom I have a lot in common. We're both wildly energetic, very positive, and truly love teaching. We also both used to have way too much stuff, and packing up our classrooms at the end of the school year was quite a process. It took us both longer than we would have liked.

It was difficult, too, being around others that were quite efficient and quick at packing up. Well-meaning colleagues would stop by to say goodbye for the summer and might comment, "Oh, you still have quite a lot to do."

After one of those experiences, I appeared in my friend's doorway in tears. I knew I still had a lot to do. Being reminded of it had shaken me out of my can-do mindset, and I was overwhelmed.

She empathized because she'd been in that situation, too. We walked back to my classroom and looked around. She pointed out everything she could see that I had already done. It helped a lot to be able to focus on what I had done: my ta-das rather than my to-dos. We went back to her classroom and pointed out all of the things that she had done, as well. We both jumped back into packing up with a better mindset and a lighter heart.

It became an end-of-the-year tradition for us to stop by each other's rooms and say, "Wow! Look how much you have done already!" We don't even live in the same state anymore, but to this day, more than fifteen years later, one of us always texts the other sometime in June to say: "Your classroom looks great! You're almost finished!"

Communication Self-Care

Becky Wanless, coauthor of *Empowering Educators*, grades K, 1, 2

It was around 10:00 p.m. and I was getting ready to call it a night when I heard my phone ding. It was an email from a parent, who was clearly very upset over a situation that had happened at school that day. She gave few details about the situation and demanded I call her immediately. I was left wondering what she was talking about as I reread her email countless times. Needless to say, I couldn't sleep at all that night.

I arrived at school the next day bright and early, an extra-large coffee in hand, having had little sleep and feeling nervous. I took a deep breath, reminded myself to be curious, and made a call to the parent. There had been a situation at lunch that involved another student in a different class. The situation had ultimately been resolved by a lunch teacher, but it hadn't been shared with me. The parent had been taken aback when her child shared what had happened and was upset that she had not been contacted. I listened to her concerns and reassured her that I would gather more information and call her back later that day so we would both have the full story. We ended the conversation on a positive note, and later that day I was able to provide more details about what had happened.

While this situation was ultimately straightforward to resolve, I literally lost sleep over it. I'd spent ten hours in a panic, and I wasn't going to let that happen again. That was the moment I set up some healthy communication boundaries. I immediately removed my school email from my cell phone.

While it is tempting to check or respond to emails at night or make a quick parent phone call, you also need to unplug from the school day and allow yourself time and permission to recharge and take care of yourself. You spend the day giving your all to families, students, and colleagues. Whatever emails are in your inbox after the school day is done can wait.

Removing your school email from personal devices and setting clear communication boundaries with families (and colleagues) about availability can be two of the best things for your mental well-being. Here are some tips for communication self-care:

- **Communicate your hours of availability.** "I will respond to emails from 9:30 to 10:00 a.m. and from 3:30 to 4:00 p.m. I am busy teaching during other hours of the day. If you have an emergency, please call the office at . . ."
- **Let families know that you are unable to respond to emails during the evening.** "I am unable to respond to emails after 4:00 p.m. as I am spending time with my family" or "I am unable to respond to emails after 5:00 p.m., as I am likely resting and rejuvenating from a day full of joy and learning."
- **Give families a time frame in which to expect a response.** "While I try to respond to all emails in a timely manner, it might take twenty-four hours for you to receive a response."

Final Word

In the same way that we work so hard each and every day to make sure our students have what they need to be successful academically, socially, and emotionally, we also need to make sure we have the same support in place for ourselves. To best help our students, we need to take care of ourselves first. When educators are empowered to create healthy classrooms that are developmentally responsive and effectively managed, with positive communities and engaging academics, all students can succeed.

Appendix

Interactive Learning Structures

Interactive learning structures are lively, easy-to-use activities that enable students to engage more deeply with their learning by moving around, stretching their thinking, and positively interacting with their peers. These purposeful structures are designed to help students strengthen their academic, social, and emotional skills. Here are some examples of effective interactive learning structures for middle schoolers.

Think-Pair-Share or Think-Pair-Square

1. Think: Pose a question or topic for discussion to the whole class. Provide a few minutes of quiet thinking time when students work independently to jot down their responses.

2. Pair: Students pair up and share their responses.

3. Share: Reconvene the class and ask pairs to report back on their conversation. Alternatively, students can "Square," with two sets of partners forming a group of four to share their conversations.

Jigsaws

1. Name the learning goal. For example: "I have three short articles that give interesting perspectives on rock formations. You'll each read one article and then discuss it twice—first with those who have read the same article, and then with those who haven't."

2. Divide students evenly into "expert" groups. Name one facilitator per group and assign each group a short article (or section of content): groups A and B read and discuss an article on sedimentary rocks, groups C and D igneous rocks, and groups E and F metamorphic rocks. (For longer texts, assign reading ahead of time.) Offer a quick reminder about expectations: "Remember to listen respectfully to each other's ideas."

3. Give groups five minutes to read their article and another five minutes to agree on its key ideas. Each student writes down the ideas on a sheet of paper.

4. Members of each expert group count off. All ones form a "jigsaw" group, twos another, and so on. Every jigsaw group will have experts on each article.

5. In their jigsaw groups, students share the key ideas of their article and write the new information on their paper. Give reminders as needed: "How will you make sure there's time for questions and comments in your group?"

6. As a whole class, summarize the key ideas of each article to ensure that everyone has the same understanding of the content.

Four Corners

1. Name the learning goal. For example, as part of a discussion about *Dragonwings* by Laurence Yep: "You're going to dig deeper into the book's main characters to explore different aspects of each character."

2. Pose a question that has four possible responses: "In the early chapters of the book, what in your opinion is the greatest challenge Moon Shadow faces, and why?"

3. Designate one corner of the room for each response:

    ○ Corner one—His physical journey to the United States

    ○ Corner two—Leaving his mother and grandmother

    ○ Corner three—Being a new immigrant in the United States

    ○ Corner four—Discovering there is no Golden Mountain

4. Give students a minute to reflect on their choice. When time is up, they move to the corresponding corner. Reinforce positive behavior: "I noticed you carefully considered your choice before moving to that corner."

5. In their corners, students discuss in small groups (or pairs) why they made their choice and provide reasons and evidence to support their decision.

6. Allow about 30 seconds for each person to share or 1–2 minutes in total for a more free-flowing discussion. Provide a 10-second warning before time is up.

7. Repeat, with a new question and responses, as time allows.

Maître d'

1. Name the learning goal. For example: "You're going to form different table sizes [standing groups] to share ideas about our unit on healthy living."

2. Remind students about the expectations for forming new table groups, emphasizing the importance of being inclusive, friendly, and respectful: "What will you do to make sure everyone is included?" (If needed, model how to move about the room safely.)

3. Call out a grouping, starting with "Table for two." Students quickly form pairs of their own choosing (with one table of three, if needed).

4. Ask a question to focus the discussion: "How might you increase your weekly physical activity?" Give students 1–2 minutes to share (with a 15-second warning). Reinforce positive behavior: "I heard a lot of encouraging words when people got stuck on an idea to share."

5. Call out "Table for three," have students form new groups, and ask the same question or a new one. After groups have discussed this question, call out "Table for four." Repeat as time allows, continuing to vary the table numbers.

6. To extend the learning, bring everyone back together and ask a few volunteers to share highlights from one of their conversations.

Interactive Modeling

Interactive Modeling is an effective way to teach any routine or skill that needs to be done in one specific way, perhaps for safety, efficiency, or other reasons.

Steps of Middle School Interactive Modeling

1. Describe what you will model and why.
2. Model the behavior while students notice.
3. Give students the opportunity to collaborate and practice.
4. Reinforce practice with immediate feedback.

Example of Middle School Interactive Modeling

1. **Describe what you will model and why.**
   "Today, I'm going to show you how to handle the microscope you'll be using in our cellular respiration unit. This will help you complete your experiment and keep our equipment in good shape."

2. **Model the behavior while students notice.**
   As students watch, walk over to where the microscopes are kept. Retrieve the microscope, handling it slowly and carefully so what you're doing is clear to observers. Carefully bring the microscope to the lab table and set it up in the space.

3. **Give students the opportunity to collaborate and practice.**
   "Now, you're going to have a few minutes to talk to your table group. What did you notice me doing?" After a few minutes, ask volunteers to share what their group discussed. Record answers if appropriate. Ask questions to fill in any missing pieces ("What did I do with the microscope after I put it down on the table?"). After the discussion, give students the opportunity to practice with the real microscopes.

4. **Reinforce practice with immediate feedback.**
   Walk around the room as students practice and offer feedback about what you observe. "I see students carrying the microscope with both hands. That's showing care with this important equipment." Discreetly offer any reminders that are needed. "Alex, remember to put one hand under the base."

Logical Consequences vs. Punishment

When students need support to help get their behavior back on track, teachers might choose to use a logical consequence. Unlike punishments, logical consequences are respectful of students, realistic to carry out, and relevant to the misbehavior.

	Punishment	Logical Consequences
Intention	To ensure compliance by using external controls that make the student feel ashamed or bad in other ways	To help students recognize the effects of their actions and develop internal controls
Underlying belief	Students will do better only because they fear punishment and will seek to avoid it	Students will want to do better and can do better with reflection and practice
Teacher's approach and tone	Reacts automatically with little thought; voice is angry and punitive	Gathers more information before reacting; voice is calm and matter-of-fact
Nature of the consequence	Not related to the behavior or the damage done; not reasonable for the student to do	Related to the behavior; reasonable for the student to do
Message to the student	The student is the problem	The damage done, not the student, is the problem

Responsive Advisory Meeting

The purpose-driven format of Responsive Advisory Meeting enables students to experience the full power of Advisory and enables schools to meet all the objectives of a strong Advisory program.

Ideally, Responsive Advisory Meeting takes place at a regular time each day (or most days) for about 20 minutes. This length of time allows students to move through all four Responsive Advisory Meeting components and have meaningful conversations and interactions with their peers and advisor.

In schools that don't yet have a devoted time for Advisory or that have limited time scheduled, teachers can adapt Responsive Advisory Meeting to use during a few minutes of homeroom time or before class.

Each of the four components of Responsive Advisory Meeting plays an essential role in creating positive energy, engagement, and feelings of mutual respect and belonging. The four components are:

Arrival welcome—The advisor welcomes each student by name as they enter the classroom.

Announcements—In advance, the advisor writes an interactive message and displays it where it can be easily seen and read by all students.

Acknowledgments—In pairs or small groups, students share their responses to a prompt in the announcement message, a piece of news about themselves, or ideas about a topic related to their studies or interests.

Activity—The whole group does a fun, lively activity that's focused on the specific purpose of the meeting.

Each meeting concludes with a question or statement that prompts student reflection on the meeting's purpose.

For more information, see *The Responsive Advisory Meeting Book* (Center for Responsive Schools 2018).

Booklists for Diverse and Inclusive Classroom Libraries

What our students read is a way to show they exist. It's essential that any library contain materials that reflect both our students and the world around them. The material we choose for our class libraries can also both engage and connect to the timely, real-world issues students care about. These booklists provide a starting point for building a diverse and inclusive classroom library:

- American Library Association, Inclusive Booklists
  https://www.ala.org/advocacy/literacy/inclusive-booklists

- American Library Association, Recommended Reading: Celebrating Diversity
  https://libguides.ala.org/c.php?g=488238&p=3530814

- Lee and Low Books, Multicultural and Diverse Books for Grades 6–8
  https://www.leeandlow.com/middle-school

- GreatSchools.org
  https://www.greatschools.org/gk/book-lists/8-books-that-celebrate-diversity-for-tweens/

Sample Parent Communications

Use these sample messages as a jumping-off point for your own routine communications, as well as messages sharing positive noticings and acknowledging challenges. These samples can be adapted to reflect your language, voice, and style.

Positive Noticings:

"I wanted to share with you how well _____ did on our most recent class project. They have made such progress as a collaborator this year, and I was so impressed to see how tactfully they balanced their own ideas with their peers' input. Group work can be tricky sometimes, but _____'s clever sense of humor helps keep the work enjoyable. It's been such a joy to teach _____ this year!"

"Today, I noticed something special and I wanted to make sure you knew about it. I watched as _____ noticed a new student trying to make sense of their complicated schedule and school map. They took extra time to show compassion, explain the directions, and walk them over to the class, promising to check in with them later. The relief on the other student's face was priceless."

Acknowledging Challenges:

"As we discussed earlier in the year, we have been keeping an eye on your _____'s frustration level with their work. Lately, as the complexity of the work increases, I've noticed their frustration level becomes elevated. In keeping with our partnership, let's plan a time to meet to brainstorm next steps that set them up to be successful during the last trimester. When would be a good time next week to connect?"

"Last week, _____ made a commitment to turn in any outstanding work in order to catch up with their learning targets. At this point, they are on track to lower their overall grade in the class. The model of mastery we have means the actual learning is more important than the physical work.

When we talked, _____ said it would help to have a brainstorm session with you tonight to come up with some creative ways they can demonstrate their learning. Let me know what you come up with. I look forward to working with _____ to implement their ideas!"

Routine Classroom Updates:

Greetings, Seventh Grade Families,

As we progress through the school year, we will make many transitions from subject to subject as we explore seventh grade science. We have just successfully completed our unit on the solar system, and our room decorations look out of this world! I wish to thank you all for your support on your child's solar system project this past week.

We are now moving into our unit on life science, and our goal is to have all students create a model of the cell using regular household items. Hands-on models like these help your child better understand the parts of a cell and the function of these parts. Next week, your child will complete a project-planning guide to start thinking about the cell model project, so please be on the lookout for that.

If you have any questions about our upcoming projects and efforts, please let me know.

Dear Families,

Here's a quick weekly update to let you know what we're up to in math class.

Past: Completed our unit on graphing on the coordinate plane last week

Now: Started a new unit this week on transformations on the coordinate plane

Looking ahead: Next week's focus is on getting more comfortable with the different types of transformations

Upcoming events: Math vocabulary quiz coming up next Friday

What you can do: Check in with your child about how they're feeling with the new material and make sure they have accessed the quiz review materials on the online portal

As always, please feel free to be in touch with any questions.

Happy Thursday, Sixth Grade Families!

This is a quick update on your sixth grader's social studies class. Tomorrow marks the end of our World War I unit, and we are getting ready to transition to World War II. Please take a look at [insert grading communication tool or say attached document] to see what assignments remain missing. They can be turned in until [insert date]. If you have any questions as we move into our next unit, please let me know.

References

Ahmed, Sara K. 2019. *Being the Change: Lessons and Strategies to Teach Social Comprehension*. Portsmouth, NH: Heinemann.

American Federation of Teachers and Badass Teachers Association. 2017. *2017 Educator Quality of Work Life Survey*. Washington, DC: American Federation of Teachers. https://www.aft.org/sites/default/files/2017_eqwl_survey_web.pdf.

Center for Development of Human Services, SUNY Buffalo State. 2015. *Child Development Guide*. New York State Office of Children and Family Services.

Diliberti, Melissa Kay, Heather L. Schwartz, and David Grant. 2021. *Stress Topped the Reasons Why Public School Teachers Quit, Even Before COVID-19*. Santa Monica, CA: RAND Corporation. https://www.rand.org/pubs/research_reports/RRA1121-2.html.

Dumas, Michael J., and Joseph Derrick Nelson. 2016. "(Re)Imagining Black Boyhood: Toward a Critical Framework for Educational Research." *Harvard Educational Review* 86, no. 1 (Spring): 27–47.

Epstein, Rebecca, Jamilia J. Blake, and Thalia González. 2017. *Girlhood Interrupted: The Erasure of Black Girls' Childhood*. Washington, DC: Georgetown Law Center on Poverty and Inequality. https://dx.doi.org/10.2139/ssrn.3000695.

Gallup. 2014. *State of America's Schools: A Path to Winning Again in Education*. Washington, DC: Gallup. http://www.gallup.com/services/178709/state-america-schools-report.aspx.

Goddard, Roger, Yvonne Goddard, Eun Sook Kim, and Robert Miller. 2015. "A Theoretical and Empirical Analysis of the Roles of Instructional Leadership, Teacher Collaboration, and Collective Efficacy Beliefs in Support of Student Learning." *American Journal of Education* 121, no. 4: 501–530.

Hattie, John. Mindframes and Maximizers. 3rd Annual Visible Learning Conference, Washington, DC, July 2016.

Jones, Stephanie M., and Suzanne M. Bouffard. 2012. "Social and Emotional Learning in Schools: From Programs to Strategies and Commentaries." *Social Policy Report* 26, no. 4 (Winter): 1–33.

Kirwan Institute for the Study of Race and Ethnicity. Implicit Bias Module Series. 2018. The Ohio State University, the Center for the Study of Social Policy, and the Schott Foundation for Public Education. https://kirwaninstitute.osu.edu/implicit-bias-training.

National Education Association. 2021. "Racial Justice." EdJustice. https://neaedjustice.org/social-justice-issues/racial-justice/.

PBLWorks. n.d. "'Doing a Project' vs. Project Based Learning." pblworks.org/doing-project-vs-project-based-learning

Pink, Daniel H. 2011. *Drive: The Surprising Truth About What Motivates Us*. New York: Penguin.

Project Implicit. 2011. "Implicit Association Test." https://implicit.harvard.edu/implicit/takeatest.html.

Wood, Chip. 2017. *Yardsticks: Child and Adolescent Development Ages 4–14*. 4th ed. Turners Falls, MA: Center for Responsive Schools.

Further Resources

All the practices recommended in this book come from or are consistent with the *Responsive Classroom* approach to teaching—an evidence-based education approach associated with greater teacher effectiveness, higher student achievement, and improved school climate. *Responsive Classroom* practices help educators build competencies in four interrelated domains: engaging academics, positive community, effective management, and developmentally responsive teaching.

To learn more, see the following resources published by Center for Responsive Schools and available at www.responsiveclassroom.org.

Building an Academic Community: The Middle School Teacher's Guide to the First Four Weeks of the School Year. From *Responsive Classroom* with Ellie Cornecelli and Amber Searles. 2018.

Make Learning Meaningful: How to Leverage the Brain's Natural Learning Cycle in K–8 Classrooms by Kristen Vincent. 2021.

Middle School Motivators: 22 Interactive Learning Structures. From *Responsive Classroom*. 2016.

The Power of Our Words for Middle School: Teacher Language That Helps Students Learn. From *Responsive Classroom*. 2016.

Refocus and Recharge: 50 Brain Breaks for Middle Schoolers. From *Responsive Classroom*. 2016.

The Responsive Advisory Meeting Book: 150+ Purposeful Plans for Middle School. From *Responsive Classroom* with Michelle Benson, Rio Clemente, Nicole Doner, Jeannie Holenko, Dana Januszka, and Amber Searles. 2018.

Seeing the Good in Students: A Guide to Classroom Discipline in Middle School. From *Responsive Classroom* with Rashid Abdus-Salaam, Andy Moral, and Kathleen Wylie. 2019.

Strengthening the Parent-Teacher Partnership by Jane Cofie. 2021.

Yardsticks: Child and Adolescent Development Ages 4–14, 4th edition, by Chip Wood. 2017.

Yardsticks Guide Series: Common Developmental Characteristics in the Classroom and at Home, Grades K–8. From *Responsive Classroom*, 2018; based on *Yardsticks* by Chip Wood.

Index

active teaching, 99–100
   in eighth grade, 122–123
   as part of lesson design, sixth grade, 104, 106–107
   in seventh grade, 114–115
assessments
   in eighth grade, 124–125
   formative, sixth grade, 107–108

break it, fix it, 40
   use of, seventh grade, 56–57

C.A.R.E.S. social and emotional competencies, 169
   adult traits of, 172–173
   and CASEL competencies, 169
child and adolescent development, key principles of, 10–11
class meetings, eighth grade, 92
classroom displays
   in eighth grade, 62
   in seventh grade, 54
   in sixth grade, 45–46
classroom organization
   in eighth grade, 60–61
   in seventh grade, 52–53
   in sixth grade, 43–45
closing circle, and positive community in seventh grade, 84
culturally responsive teaching, 92–93, 100–101
   and communicating with families, eighth grade, 158–161
   and "equity intelligence," eighth grade, 126–127
   and lesson design, seventh grade, 117–119

developmental characteristics
   and school implications, eighth graders (table), 33–34
   and school implications, seventh graders (table), 25–26
   and school implications, sixth graders (table), 18–19
discipline
   as part of effective management, 38
   as part of positive community, 72–73

diversity
   in classroom displays, sixth grade, 45–46
   in classroom library, eighth grade, 62
envisioning language, 72
   and group identity, seventh grade, 58
   and positive community, seventh grade, 87
families
   beginning-of-the-year survey for, eighth grade, 152–153
   building positive relationships with, 133–134
   connecting virtually with, seventh grade, 149–150
   regular communication with, sixth grade, 137
   special concerns of, seventh grade, 137–139
   special concerns of, sixth grade, 145–147

grades, communicating with families about in sixth grade, 138
guiding principles, *Responsive Classroom*, 2

implicit bias, 179–180
interactive learning structures
   incorporating into daily schedule, sixth grade, 47
   as part of interactive learning, sixth grade, 79–80
   and social and emotional learning, seventh grade, 24
   and social and emotional learning, sixth grade, 17
Interactive Modeling
   as part of teaching routines, eighth grade, 65
   and teaching academic behaviors, eighth grade, 32
   teaching routines with, seventh grade, 22–23
   teaching routines with, sixth grade, 47

lesson design
   and project-based learning, eighth grade, 120–122
   in seventh grade, 105–106
   steps of, sixth grade, 103–104
   three-part structure of, 98–99

logical consequences, 39–41. *See also* break it, fix it; loss of privilege; Space and Time
    vs. punishment, 40
loss of privilege, 40, 66–67

Maze Game, 16
mistakes, learning from
    in eighth grade, 65–66
    in sixth grade, 15–17

natural learning cycle, 98
nonverbal signals, eighth grade, 64

observation
    of other classrooms, 187–188
    of students, sixth grade, 107–108

parent-teacher conferences
    in sixth grade, 139–141
    virtual, seventh grade, 149–150
project-based learning, eighth grade, 120–123
punishment
    and issues of inequity, 40
    vs. logical consequences, 40

redirecting language
    and positive community, seventh grade, 87–89
reinforcing language
    and positive community, eighth grade, 93–95
reminding language
    and positive community, sixth grade, 76–77
responding to misbehavior
    and classroom management, eighth grade, 65–67
    and classroom management, seventh grade, 55–57
    and classroom management, sixth grade, 49–51
Responsive Advisory Meeting
    building positive community with, 71
    multiple language greetings in, eighth grade, 159
    in seventh grade, 81–82

routines and procedures, 38–39
    in eighth grade, 62–65
    modeling, seventh grade, 22–23
    in sixth grade, 46–48
    teaching with colleagues, 48
rules
    investing students in, eighth grade, 91–93
    investing students in, seventh grade, 85–86
    investing students in, sixth grade, 49–51, 77–78

schedules
    in eighth grade, 62–63
    in seventh grade, 55
    in sixth grade, 46–47
self-care, teacher, 190–196
social and emotional learning
    in adults, 166–171
    in eighth grade, 31
    in seventh grade, 24
    in sixth grade, 17
    and teacher belief domains, 182–183
Social and Emotional Type Inventory, 171
Space and Time, 45
    teaching as a routine, sixth grade, 48
stress, teacher, 163–164

teacher belief domains, 182–183
teacher language, 42, 71. *See also* envisioning language; redirecting language; reinforcing language; reminding language
    and classroom management, sixth grade, 50–51
    developmental considerations for, seventh grade, 87
    on first day of school, sixth grade, 79
    and high expectations, sixth grade, 74–75
    silence as part of, sixth grade, 75
teacher leadership, 175–178
    styles of, 178

voice and choice, eighth grade, 29, 31

About the Publisher

Center for Responsive Schools, Inc., a not-for-profit educational organization, offers professional development, curriculum, and books and resources to support academic, social, and emotional learning.

Center for Responsive Schools (CRS) is the developer of *Responsive Classroom*®, a research-based education approach associated with greater teacher effectiveness, higher student achievement, and improved school climate, and of Fly Five, a comprehensive social-emotional learning curriculum for kindergarten through eighth grade.

CRS Publishing, the independent publishing arm of Center for Responsive Schools, creates inspiring yet practical books for educators and students to support growth, learning, and success in and out of school.

Center for Responsive Schools' vision is to influence and inspire a world-class education for every student in every school, every day, and to bring hope and joy to educators and students alike. Visit us at crslearn.org to learn more: